OF THE MATERIALS INTERIOR DESIGN

A compendium of interior designer's materials consisting of Area and Oriental Rugs and Carpet; Draperies, Curtains, Shades, Shutters and Woven Blinds; Acrylic, Upholstered and Wood Furniture; Textiles, Wall Coverings and the methods by which they are manufactured and constructed.

By Dennis Grant Murphy, ASID

STRATFORD HOUSE PUBLISHING COMPANY

First Edition
Tenth Printing
Printed in the United States

LIBRARY OF CONGRESS CATALOG NO. 211-196
ISBN NO. 0-938614-00-2

TO MICHELE, MICHAEL, CAROL, GRANT,
JEAN AND DENISE — MY CHILDREN

ACKNOWLEDGEMENTS

Gladys Nobel Murphy
Editor

Henry Cartier Durand, Designer

Jamie Roach, Illustrator

Bonnie Clyde, Supplementary Illustrations

The author and publisher wish to extend their sincere appreciation to the following individuals who generously provided their expertise for the development of this book:

Glenn Albright; James Beisner; Vi Benbassat; Max Bobrosky; A. Allen Dizik, FASID; Tom Gast; Carroll Hassell; Jules Heumann; Charles Hollis Jones; Barbara Jenks; King Karpen; Roz Lev; Nancy McCarthy; Adam Newmar; Mary Popejoy; Larry Schneider; Philip Sicola; Helen Webber; David Wilson

FOREWORD

The interior furnishings industry has undergone many changes during the past ten years, and I can say without reservation that at no time have we had such a diversification of fine designer products as we have today. These products are a result of the development and application of new materials coupled with new manufacturing techniques. They were brought about by the demand for better quality merchandise and the competition among the manufacturers to supply this merchandise. Needless to say, they are a benefit to both the designer and the client.

The designer must have a thorough knowledge of these materials in order to use them to the greatest advantage. However, it has been my experience, during the quarter century that I have been a member of the interior design profession, that many texts dealing with interior design products are inadequate. Whenever I wanted to research a particular subject, it was often necessary to use five or six books in order to obtain the salient facts. Moreover, it was even more difficult to find information concerning the construction and manufacture of furnishings pertinent to my needs.

Since it would be useful as well as more convenient to have all the essential information in a single book, the idea for *The Materials of Interior Design* was developed.

This book deals with interior furnishings only; specifically, their composition, construction and useability. It was written to provide the designer with a better understanding of the materials that are required for the creation of a product and how they are assembled. It refers to those furnishings, in particular, that meet the level of quality demanded by the profession, and it will allow the designer to use these products intelligently so that they will perform according to specification.

I would like to remind the reader that decorative building materials have been intentionally omitted from the contents of this book. They should be considered a separate topic as they are items which are usually affixed to a structure and are normally supplied by contractors even though they are often specified by interior designers.

The Materials of Interior Design consists of facts about materials and construction, not opinions. I feel it is the reader's prerogative to make any decisions about which of these elements he feels are best. He alone knows the client and the requirements of the design project, so he alone must make the selections and specifications.

I should like to point out that the book is concise and descriptive for ease of understanding. (For this I cannot take full credit as the editor is an ardent believer in simplicity.) Also, the text has definitions for the terms used and historical backgrounds of the different types of furnishings. There are many drawings and photographs to illustrate the ideas and techniques.

The research for the text covered a three year period and included interviews with some of most knowledgeable people in the furnishings industry. Because of their cooperation and enthusiasm for the subject, the tasks of those associated with the book were a pleasure. The Materials of Interior Design would never have come into being if it had not been for their interest and expertise.

DENNIS GRANT MURPHY
October, 1978

PART I

CHAPTER 1   **WOODS**   13

Definition of Wood   14

Characteristics of Wood   14

Species of Wood   14

Types of Wooden Materials   17

Joints and Joint Supports   20

Fasteners   22

Wood Finishing   23

       Definition of Finishing   23

       Finishing Processes   24

CHAPTER 2   **TEXTILES**   31

Definition and History of Textiles   32

Fiber   33

       Definition of Fiber   33

       Types of Fiber   33

Yarn   41

       Definition of Yarn   41

       Fibers Used in Yarn   42

Weaving   42

       Definition and History of Weaving   42

       Types of Weaves   43

       Types of Woven Fabric   46

Knitting   51

       Definition and History of Knitting   51

       Knitting Stitches   52

       Knit Fabric Construction   52

       Types of Knitted Fabric   52

Braiding   53

       Definition of Braiding   53

       Types of Braided Fabric   53

Fabric Finishing   54

       Definition of Finishing   54

       Types of Finishing   54

CHAPTER 3   PLASTICS   63

Definition of Plastic   64
Groups of Plastics   64
    Thermosetting   64
    Thermoplastic   64
Methods of Fabrication   65
    Casting and Molding   65
    Forming   66
Coloring   66
Construction   66
    Polishing   66
    Fastening   67
Plastic Materials   67
    Laminate   67
    Resin Board   68

PART II

CHAPTER 4   WALL COVERINGS   71

Definition and History of Wall Coverings   72
Color and Design   74
Wall Covering Surfaces   75
Types of Wall Coverings   76
Sizes of Wall Coverings   79
Lining   79
Adhesives   79
Quantity of Covering   80
Installation   81

CHAPTER 5   FLOOR COVERINGS: CARPETS AND RUGS   83

Definition and History of Carpets and Rugs   84
Fibers   87
Color   87
Carpet and Rug Construction   89
Methods of Manufacturing   90
    Weaving   90
    Knitting   91
    Tufting   91
Backing   92
Cushion   93
Installation   93

CHAPTER 6   WINDOW COVERINGS: DRAPERIES AND CURTAINS   99

Definition and History of Draperies and Curtains   100
Styles of Window Coverings   101
Hardware   105
Construction   106
Installation   111
Workrooms   111

WINDOW COVERINGS: SHADES   113

Definition of Window Shades   114
Styles   114
Fabrics   116
Colors   116
Measurements   116
Hardware   117

WINDOW COVERINGS: BLINDS   119

Definition of Blinds   120
Styles   120
Framing   120
Color   120
Components   121
Measurements   122

WINDOW COVERINGS: WOVEN SHADES   123

Definition of Woven Shades   124
Styles   124
Construction   127
Colors   127
Installation   127

WINDOW COVERINGS: SHUTTERS   129

Definition of Shutters   130
Styles   130
Construction   130
Hardware   131
Colors   131
Installation   131
Measurements   133

PART III

CHAPTER 7   WOOD FURNITURE   137

History of Wood Furniture   138
Definition   145
Construction   145
     Base or Plinth   145
     Legs, Posts, Rails, Stretchers   145
     Cases   146
     Doors   149
     Drawers   151
     Trays   151
     Shelves   152
     Tops   152
     Cornices   153
Hardware   153
Chairs   154
The Custom Shop   155

CHAPTER 8   UPHOLSTERED FURNITURE   159

Definition and History of Upholstered Furniture   161
Frames   163
Operations   165
     Webbing   166
     Springing   167
     Rubber Webbing   170
     Burlapping   171
     Edging   171
     Stuffing   172
     Casing   173
     Padding   173
     Channeling   173
     Tufting   174
     Seats   175
     Arms   177
     Wings   178

Backs   178
Coverings   179
Cushions and Pillows   185
Loose Cushion Upholstery   188
Recovering   188
Restyling   188
The Custom Upholstery Shop   189

CHAPTER 9   **ACRYLIC FURNITURE**   193
History of Acrylic Furniture   194
Definition of Acrylic Resin   195
Construction   196
Features   196
Molded Plastic Furniture   197

BIBLIOGRAPHY   198
INDEX   199
CREDITS FOR PHOTOGRAPHS   205

PART I

CHAPTER 1 — **WOODS**
CHAPTER 2 — **TEXTILES**
CHAPTER 3 — **PLASTICS**

CHAPTER 1   **WOODS**

Definition of Wood
Characteristics of Wood
      Color
      Grain
      Hardness
      Strength
Species of Wood
Types of Wooden Materials
      Solid Wood
      Veneer
      Molding
      Plywood
      Laminates
      Cane
Joints and Joint Supports
Fasteners
Wood Finishing
      Definition of Finishing
      Finishing Processes
      Preparation of the Surface
      Coloring
      Filling
      Films
      Rubbing
      Polishing
      Painting

WOODS

WOOD, according to Webster, is "the hard fibrous substance beneath the bark in the stems and branches of trees and shrubs." It is a tough organic material that produces a firm, solid form, yet it shapes easily and is readily worked. It has many types and varieties, each with its own characteristics.

CHARACTERISTICS OF WOOD

The characteristics which individualize woods and make them attractive include color, grain, hardness, and strength.

COLOR is the shade of the "raw" wood before it has been treated with any finishing agents.

GRAIN is the design in the wood made by the layers of fibers and the size and arrangement of the pores. The fibers are stacked in layers and interspersed with the pores. The PORES are the openings through which fluids are absorbed or discharged. They may be small and compactly distributed, producing CLOSE-GRAIN wood, or they may be large and widely-dispersed for OPEN-GRAIN wood.

The pattern of the fibers makes the FIGURE of the grain. Different figures may be obtained from the same type of wood by cutting the wood from several directions; by using all sections of a tree, especially deformed or abnormal areas; by making cuts from species that have a distinction between the density and color of the wood during the spring and summer seasons; and by exposing the rays, curly grain, or ends of the wood as it is cut. These cuts are made with great care as grain is very important. It is the attribute that makes wood interesting and gives it a pleasing appearance.

HARDNESS is the capacity of the wood to resist abuse.

STRENGTH is the inherent resilience of the wood against force and stress.

SPECIES OF WOOD

There are many varieties of wood available; however, only particular species are practical for the manufacture of furniture. These are mahogany, rosewood, teak, ebony, walnut, oak, maple, red gum, orientalwood, satinwood, myrtle burls, cherry, sugar knotty pine, pecan or hickory, and some exotic woods that have special features.

MAHOGANY is extensively used in both solid and veneer form. African mahogany has a variety of figures from straight stripe to mottled or fiddleback with large swirls and crotches. West Indian mahogany has a close grain and a silky texture. American mahogany has a straight grain with a compact texture. This wood is soft enough to be easily worked into a design, yet it is hard enough to withstand shocks. It takes stains well, and it is usually finished with a light reddish-brown or brown stain that brings out the figure, although bleached and natural effects are also used. It will receive any type of finish with good results and may be polished or dull rubbed.

ROSEWOOD is an ornamental wood found principally in Brazil. It has a peculiar growth feature in that the heartwood starts to decay before the tree is mature. By the time the tree is felled the center is hollow and the wood can only be cut in half-round flitches. The wood color runs from red to brown, and it is streaked with black lines of resin. The pores are variable in size and are irregularly and sparsely distributed. They are extremely oily and must be filled, usually with a light red filler. The wood is left natural, although it may be stained; and it will take a fine polish. The resinous nature of this wood makes it difficult to work, and it must be finished carefully.

TEAK has white sapwood and golden yellow heartwood in the young tree, but when the heartwood is seasoned, it changes to a brown mottled with dark streaks. A pleasant, aromatic odor emanates from the heartwood and it retains this fragrance for many years. Teak timber is strong, of average hardness, and of medium weight. Its great durability is its principal trait and this makes it one of the most valuable woods.

EBONY cut from the D. Ebenum variety is considered the most excellent type. This tree, which grows in India and Ceylon, has a narrow trunk with black, charred-looking bark, white sapwood, and heartwood with a fine, intense black color. Calamander ebony, also from Ceylon, has a close grain, great hardness, and a hazel brown color that is mottled and striped with black. Jamaican or American ebony is produced from a tree or shrub which has a trunk that seldom grows more than four inches in diameter. The heartwood has a rich dark brown color, great weight, and exceptional hardness. Because of its color, durability, hardness, and ability to accept a high polish, ebony wood is used for cabinet work, inlaying, turned articles, veneering, and furniture.

WALNUT is also widely used in solid and veneer work. American black walnut varies in color from light, creamy sapwood to warm grays and light brown. Its pores are irregular but large in size and evenly distributed. It has a wide range of figures including burl, crotch, stumpwood, plain stripe, and highly figured longwood. Its texture is medium hard, but it can be worked easily. The close, even grain lends itself to carving, and its shock resistance and bending strength allow sturdy legs, rails, posts, and stretchers to be cut. It may be bleached, given a natural finish, or lightly stained. Pores may be left open or filled with a filler that is lighter or darker than the wood. It may be polished to a high gloss or dull rubbed.

OAK has a color spread from white to light and reddish brown. Its pores are large in the spring wood and decrease abruptly in summer wood. It has an unusually large ray extending from the center to the bark. It is a rather hard wood, making it difficult to work. The pores may be filled, partly filled, or left open, and it readily accepts a finish.

MAPLE is cut from American or Canadian forests of sugar, hard, or rock maple trees. It is light pink to reddish brown in color. It has very small regular pores that require no filling and a hard texture that makes it difficult to work. Its logs are highly figured and yield fiddleback, blister, curly, and bird's-eye grains. The close grain and hardness of this wood prevent stains from penetrating well; however, it may be stained as well as bleached or left natural. It will take any type of finish and may be dull rubbed or rubbed to a fine satin gloss.

RED GUM has reddish brown heartwood and grayish white sapwood. It has very small pores and a smooth surface, but the texture is very soft. It does not hold up well under hard use as it dents and warps easily. A filler is not required, and all types of stain penetrate well, although it is usually stained to resemble other woods.

ORIENTALWOOD is a unique timber from Queensland, Australia. Its color is brown with an overcast of salmon, green, gray, and sometimes black bindings. The figure ranges from plain stripe to mottled fiddleback and roll, and the pores are medium size, fairly uniform, and evenly distributed. It is generally given an amber stain, a light brown filler, and a polished surface.

SATINWOOD comes from Ceylon, India, and the West Indies. It has a silk sheen and a golden yellow color that mellows with age. The wood has a fine, even texture, and the grain runs in narrow parallel bandings. The pores are indistinct and filled with a gummy substance that does not show after the wood is finished. It needs only a small amount of filler. It is often given a natural finish or stained light brown or orange-yellow.

MYRTLE BURLS are cut from California and Oregon trees in which the plainwood, stumpwood, and burl figures have unusual designs. The pores are numerous and regularly distributed; these finish as highlights that make the wood more attractive. This wood is usually given a natural finish with a light brown filler and a dull or polished sheen.

CHERRY wood is light to dark reddish brown in color. The pores are rather close; the grain has a very slight figure; and the texture is medium hard. All stains are accepted well, but those of a reddish cast do exceptionally well. The close grain will take varnishes easily, and the surface can be rubbed to a high gloss.

SUGAR-KNOTTY PINE is popular because of its knotty appearance. This wood has a very soft texture and is generally made into veneer for hardcore plywood. There is very little figure in the grain, and the pores are close together. The wood is whitish or cream-colored so it looks well with a natural finish, although it is also painted.

PECAN or HICKORY has a reddish brown color that is often accented with dark streaks. The grain has very little figure, and the pores are small and require only slight filling. It has a hard, strong texture which makes it very durable.

Other woods which may be used occasionally or for exceptional pieces are Japanese and Korean ash; American aspen and birch; African avadire, bubinga, sapeli, tigerwood, and zebrawood; Philippine narra and paldao; and prima vera.

TYPES OF WOODEN MATERIALS

Many kinds of pieces are produced when a log is converted into lumber. These pieces may be used in their natural state or they may be put together to form special materials. Some of the materials particularly suited for furniture construction are solid wood, veneer, molding, plywood, laminates, and cane webbing.

SOLID WOOD is cut entirely from a single log. It is strong and durable; therefore, it is usually used to make the structural parts of furniture. It is not a practical substance for all parts as it warps easily and has an expansion/contraction problem. Also, it is in limited supply and, as a consequence, is expensive.

VENEER is a thin sheet or layer of fine or costly wood that is cut from a log or part of a log called a FLITCH, and VENEERING is the technique of gluing this sheet to a plain, stable groundwood.

Historically, the art of veneering is an ancient craft that has survived from pre-Egyptian times. Veneers were originally cut by hand with a multiple-blade saw. The nineteenth century witnessed the perfection of the power saw, and the whirling circular blades were able to slice the wood easily into thin sheets. Today, special cutting knives shave veneer on the flat, quarter, or half-round and produce materials less than an inch thick. The standard thickness for veneer is one-twenty-eighth inch. Some may be as thick as one-sixteenth inch or as thin as one-sixtieth inch.

Special veneers are cut from the unusual parts of the tree.

BURL VENEERS, sliced from the thickened, twisted fibers of the burl, show a beautiful peacock-tail pattern.

BUTT or STUMP VENEERS have a wavy, rippled marking.

CROTCH VENEERS, taken from the twisted fibers below the fork, have a swirl design.

Two or more pieces of veneer fitted together and glued onto a base of common material yields a veneer surface. Only woods with superior color, figure, matching possibilities, grain, and general appearance are selected for this purpose. Since similar designs and grains are on all the surfaces, many patterns are possible.

SLIP MATCHED VENEERS are sheets joined side-by-side to make it look as if the pattern is repeated.

BOOK MATCHED VENEERS have the adjacent pieces of the flitch fastened side-by-side like the open pages of a book.

DIAMOND MATCHED VENEERS use four pieces cut diagonally from the same material and fitted together to form a diamond.

REVERSE DIAMOND MATCHED VENEERS also show a diamond, but they are fitted together exactly opposite to the diamond matched.

CHECKERBOARD MATCHED VENEERS give each piece a one-quarter turn so that a checkerboard effect is produced.

FOUR-WAY CENTER AND BUTT MATCHED VENEERS join four pieces side-to-side and end-to-end.

Veneers may be cut into small pieces of various shapes and sizes so that special designs and pictures can be created. The term describing the procedure for this type of woodworking is called inlay. The art of INLAY recesses veneers of contrasting woods into solid or veneer-surfaced wood that has been gouged out in the same pattern. Inlay may be produced through several methods.

MARQUETRY is a versatile form of inlay that permits elaborate and intricate designs to be put together. Each piece of the pattern is cut individually and then the sections are glued onto a groundwork.

PARQUETRY is an inlay form characterized by a repeated geometric design. It is built up of blocks or individual elements which are assembled into patterns that move continuously and consistently across the groundwork.

BANDING is a form of inlay in which strips or strings are set in around the edges of a piece as ornamentation.

MOLDING is a strip of shaped or carved wood that is used both decoratively and practically. It may be attached to the exteriors of doors and drawers and the edges of cabinetwork to give a finished appearance to an item and to enrich its design. It can change a simple case into a piece of furniture with a particular style. Molding may also be installed vertically or horizontally to serve as drawer or door pulls. It is fastened in place with nails, staples, as well as glue.

PLYWOOD is a manufactured wood with three or more plies or pieces glued together, one atop the other, to form a panel. The grain of each ply is set at right angles to the one above it. This type of construction makes plywood exceptionally strong both across and along the grain and reduces the natural tendency of the wood to warp and shrink with atmospheric changes. The FACE, the best surface, is a veneer, and the panel is designated by the kind of wood on its face. The other layers, the CROSSBANDS and the CORE, which gives it thickness, are made from less expensive woods.

Plywood combines the best features of its woods — the strength of sturdy, unattractive woods with the beauty of fine cabinet wood — to give an excellent material for the manufacture of furniture. It makes possible the perfect matching of grains and permits widths usually unobtainable. It allows curved effects and rounded corners, and it has a fine surface which finishes well. Its veneers have the same characteristics as the woods from which they were cut and may be stained, filled, finished, and polished to provide beautiful surfaces.

LAMINATE is another type of manufactured wood. It is built of several thin pieces that are glued together to form a single board. This method is very similar to the procedure for making plywood, the major differences being that the grain on all the pieces runs in the same direction and the pieces are usually of the same thickness.

CANE is bamboo bark that has been cut into thin strips and woven into a web. The design of the weave may be the traditional hexagonal style or a variation in the contemporary basket, small square, or rectangular shapes. Cane is used on chair seats and backs, table shelves, inserts for screens, doors, panels, etc.

JOINTS AND JOINT SUPPORTS

A JOINT is the permanent fastening of two surfaces together. The several types of joints used for wood construction are the butt, edge, rabbet, dado, lap, miter, mortise-and-tenon, and dovetail.

BUTT or PLAIN JOINTS have the square end of one piece fitted against the flat edge of the second piece. This joint will not hold up by itself; it must be reinforced with dowels. Added strength may also be supplied by a corner block.

EDGE JOINTS fasten pieces of wood together side-by-side. The grain of both parts runs parallel, but the annual rings should fall in opposite directions.

RABBET JOINTS are made by fitting one piece into the L-shaped groove cut into the other piece.

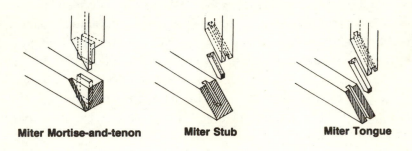

Miter Mortise-and-tenon   **Miter Stub**   **Miter Tongue**

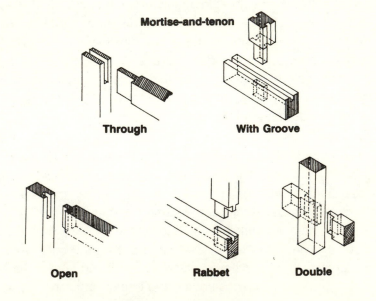

Mortise-and-tenon

Through   **With Groove**

Open   **Rabbet**   **Double**

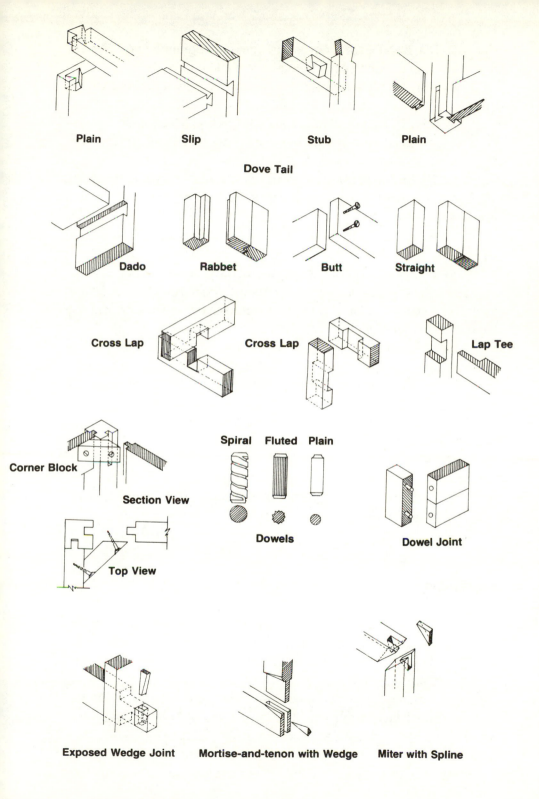

Plain

Slip

Stub

Plain

Dove Tail

Dado

Rabbet

Butt

Straight

Cross Lap

Cross Lap

Lap Tee

Corner Block

Section View

Top View

Spiral   Fluted   Plain

Dowels

Dowel Joint

Exposed Wedge Joint

Mortise-and-tenon with Wedge

Miter with Spline

DADO JOINTS are grooves cut across the grain on one piece so that the butt end of the second piece can be fitted into it.

LAP JOINTS are joints in which one member crosses over the other.

MITER JOINTS are joints cut at an angle and fitted together so that the end grain of both pieces is covered. When the pieces are attached, they form a right angle.

MORTISE-AND-TENON JOINTS have a notch or hole (mortise) cut into one piece so that a protruding edge (tenon) on the other piece can be fitted into it.

DOVETAIL JOINTS have projecting, wedge-shaped parts that fit into a corresponding cut-out space to form an interlocking joint.

In wood construction, joints are usually secured with glue, although screws are sometimes used. It may be necessary to strengthen a joint to ensure its long life and this is accomplished with dowels, splines, keys, and glue and corner blocks.

DOWELS are pins or pegs of wood, plastic, or metal that are fitted into matching holes.

SPLINES are thin pieces of wood, plywood, hardboard, or metal that are inserted in a groove between two parts of a joint.

KEYS are small pieces of wood that are inserted in a joint to hold it firmly together.

GLUE BLOCKS are small triangular or square pieces of wood used to strengthen and support two adjoining surfaces.

CORNER BLOCKS are placed at the corners of frames or the joints of legs and rails to give added strength.

FASTENERS

Straight metal fasteners are used to secure the structural sections and trims in wood furniture. SCREWS are preferred for areas that require strength. They are important for assembling structural sections, reinforcing pieces, and attaching hardware. They have good holding power, yet they do not damage the wood if they are removed or replaced. NAILS of mild steel are usually used in furniture manufacture. CASING NAILS hold well and are meant to be used in construction. Finishing nails are used in all places where the head should be concealed and for adding trim. Generally, screws and nails are not left exposed but are hidden under a wood or putty plug.

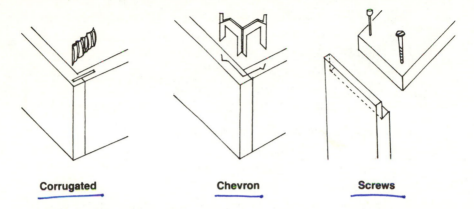

Corrugated   **Chevron**   **Screws**

MITER/JOINT fasteners are used to hold corners and joints together. CHEVRONS are arrowhead-shaped pieces of metal with varying length spikes on the bottom edge and a smooth top. They are designed to create a tight joint by drawing the wood together. CLAMP NAILS have a flat center with edges that curve out into a flange. They can be used on any joint. CORRUGATED fasteners or WIGGLE NAILS are flat nails that have been bent into a zig-zag shape. Usually, they are used to hold a miter joint together, but they can be used in any joint.

WOOD FINISHING

FINISHING is a term that encompasses all the processes used to give the desired effect to the surface of wood. When a log is cut into "raw" wood, the grain and other distinguishing marks are exposed. While these features are visible, the wood is usually a dull color and the characteristics are not pronounced. To enhance the wood and bring out its beauty, it needs to be finished.

Finishing also protects the surface of the wood. All liquids, food, and dust will stain and mar raw wood. It is impossible to remove such stains or to keep the surface clean. The surface must be sealed to maintain its natural traits and features.

Wood is affected by humidity. If the air is dry, moisture will be drawn from the wood, and if the air is damp, moisture will be absorbed by it. Constant contraction and expansion will result in permanent splitting or warping. Sealing the surface keeps the moisture out of the pores and preserves the wood.

When making articles of furniture from wood, it is often practicable to use several varieties in one piece. Sturdy woods can then be used for sections that must support other pieces, and less expensive woods can be used in unimportant areas. This would be a problem if finishing were not possible, as the piece would be a patchwork of colors. Finishing makes it possible to match all woods to each other and produce a piece of uniform color.

FINISHING PROCESSES

SURFACE PREPARATION begins the wood finishing process. Any imperfection, no matter how small, will be magnified by the finishing materials. These must be removed by sanding and filling prior to any other finishing operation.

This applies to surfaces that are to be refinished as well. REFINISHING signifies that a new surface is to be put on. It implies that an original finish will be removed entirely by some chemical or mechanical method and that the bare wood will be prepared to receive a new finish. It further implies that any necessary repairs will be made before the new finish is applied.

COLORING

Wood is a porous substance and, because of this characteristic, it has an affinity for liquids. It will absorb, to some degree, any liquid applied; and it is this absorptive quality that regulates the color of the wood. Color is an important feature for a wood product as it accents the style and design and enhances the appearance. The color should be compatible with the form and shape of the piece, but it should also be in accord with the wood itself. Wood may be finished in its natural color or it may be stained or bleached.

If a surface is finished in the shade of the raw wood, it has a NATURAL finish. No coloring agent — bleach, stain, or paint — has been applied. Some woods do not need additional color as they have beautiful color and grain that give character to the surface without further treatment.

STAIN is a dye or pigment that is used to give color to the wood. It may enhance the natural color or it may react chemically with the wood to change the color entirely. Some stains penetrate deeply to give long-lasting color; others only give superficial short-lived color that will eventually wear away. There is also a variety that will raise the grain of the wood. Types of stain include penetrating oil, wax, chemical, and varnish.

PENETRATING OIL STAIN is one of the most common types available. It is a ready-to-use stain prepared by the manufacturer by dissolving coal-tar dyes in naphtha, benzine, or turpentine. It can be used on all types of wood, but it will penetrate deeper on open-grain woods than on close-grain woods. The colors are prepared for use with particular wood types, and if they are used with other woods they will not produce the desired shade.

WATER STAIN is readily absorbed by wood, so the penetration of the stain is deep. No other type of stain can produce such a large variety of colors or colors of such brilliance and transparency. It is a coal-tar or vegetable dye available only in powder form and must be dissolved by the user in pure water solvent.

SPIRIT or ALCOHOL STAIN is made by dissolving alcohol-soluble powders in alcohol. Alcohol evaporates quickly when it is exposed to the air, so this stain dries almost immediately when it is applied to raw wood. It will penetrate an already finished surface, so it is indispensable for touch-up work. Unfortunately, the number of shades available is limited.

PIGMENT OIL STAIN is made from oil colors that are reduced to a liquid by dissolving the paste in a thinner like turpentine or benzine. Boiled linseed oil is added to bind the loose color after it has been dissolved. To hasten the drying of the stain, japan drier, a fast-drying varnish, is also added. This stain is the simplest to apply and the easiest to obtain as its ingredients are common household supplies. It is important as a blending and antiquing medium.

WAX STAIN is a preparation of penetrating oil mixed with wax and a drying agent. It brings out the true beauty of the wood, since the stain becomes part of the wood itself and gives a soft, rich wax finish.

CHEMICAL STAIN, either acid or alkaline, is indispensable in obtaining certain types of wood effects. It combines chemically with the wood, causing a reaction which colors the wood permanently. Chemical stains include permanganate of potash, lye, sal soda, acetic acid or vinegar, and ammonia.

VARNISH STAIN is a mixture of varnish and penetrating oil. This stain does not penetrate the surface and the varnish diminishes its transparency.

BLEACHING lightens the natural color of the wood and removes stains that would disfigure the finish. It decolorizes the wood through the application of chemicals, and it is an important step in preparing blond or pickled finishes.

BLOND finish requires the wood to be bleached and then finished in the natural state. Types of blond finish include blond maple, mahogany, or walnut, and natural pine.

PICKLED finish results from applying a light stain followed by a contrasting pore filler to a surface that was bleached initially. It is the distinction between the colors that produces the pickling effect. This finish is identified by its shade: oak may be limed, gray limed, and tan limed or wheat; mahogany is pickled or rose pink; and pine is pickled or driftwood gray.

FILLING

FILLING is the process of levelling the pores in the wood to make them even with the surrounding surface. FILLER, the material used in this operation, may be a paste wood type for open-grain wood or a liquid type for close-grain wood. It may be applied either before or after the wood has been stained, and it is usually the same color as the stain, unless a pickled finish is desired.

FILMS

Once the surface has been satisfactorily prepared, a transparent film should be added to protect the wood and preserve its appearance. Usually, several coats of this top film are applied so that it will be strong enough to resist shocks. Types of protective film include shellac, varnish, or lacquer as well as linseed oil and wax.

SHELLAC is one of the oldest and most widely used finishing materials. It is manufactured by dissolving lac flakes, a residue of the lac bug, in denatured alcohol. It has a fine, velvety feel that other materials cannot duplicate, and it has a durability and strength that will last indefinitely if it is properly applied and maintained. It is fast drying and becomes dust proof in only a few minutes. When used for sealing, it spreads in an even film over the surface and prevents other materials from being absorbed. As a touch-up ingredient, it becomes part of the finish and cannot be distinguished from the surrounding surface. Unfortunately, shellac is NOT waterproof, heat proof, or alcohol proof.

VARNISH is also a very old finishing material. It is a preparation made from a resinous substance that has been dissolved in oil or spirits. It flows on easily and levels evenly to give a beautiful depth and body to the finish. It does not discolor either natural or stained wood surfaces and it produces an exceptionally hard film that will be long-lasting and withstand much abuse. It has the additional properties of being waterproof, alcohol proof, and heat proof, so it can be used on all types of surfaces.

LACQUER is a relatively new finishing material as it was first developed commercially after the First World War. It is a resinous substance that has been dissolved in ethyl alcohol. It is extremely fast drying and must be applied with a spray gun. It is moisture proof, somewhat heat proof, and some types are alcohol proof. It retains its consistency and does not oxidize or change to a powder with age. Since it is clear and transparent, it will bring out the mellowness and beauty of a wood without affecting its surface. It can also be applied over surfaces that have been finished with other materials. A sealer must be applied between the lacquer and the other materials, especially varnish, paint, and penetrating oil stain. This is necessary as the lacquer will soften these undercoats and change their appearances as lacquer is also used as a finish remover.

LINSEED OIL produces a durable, waterproof, and heat-proof natural finish that has a soft, golden color. It will last indefinitely as more oil may be rubbed into the surface from time to time to keep it renewed.

RUBBING

RUBBING is the operation which removes all the imperfections such as dust, brush marks, and unevenness, from the transparent finishing material to provide a glossy appearance and a smooth feel. Abrasives are rubbed over the surface to wear away a very thin layer of the film. This must be done as quickly as possible to prevent damage to the material. The texture of abrasives differs so that many degrees of glossiness can be obtained. Steel wool and water or oil, sandpaper and water or oil, rubbing compounds, pumice stone and oil, a brush, or a machine are some of the abrasives used.

POLISHING

POLISHING implies rubbing with a tool or cloth and, usually, an abrasive paste to produce a smooth or glossy surface. Generally, the surface is thoroughly cleaned and then rubbed to a luster. Fine abrasives may be used to wear away a thin layer of the film or a light oil or a wax may be applied. Some of the polishing agents used are rottenstone, pigment oil stain, alcohol, and shellac.

OIL POLISHES are short-lived. They must be applied properly and wiped well or they will sweat and hold dust and dirt to the surface. Also, oils tend to soak through the surface and destroy the luster.

OIL MIXTURE POLISHES are preparations of several oils with wax or vinegar.

PASTE WAX POLISHES are longer-lasting because wax leaves only a very thin film on the surface. They should contain a portion of carnauba wax which will give a harder film and a higher luster. Wax enhances the natural beauty of wood, provides protection, and leaves a dry, clean surface.

ROTTENSTONE is a fine, gray powder derived from slate. When mixed with water or oil, it has unusual abrasive properties and produces a high luster when it is used as a polishing agent.

PIGMENT OIL STAIN/POLISH is the same agent used for staining except that more japan drier is added. The stain/polish should be the same color as the surface stain; it will color any surface scratches and the corners of crevices and moldings. This gives a mellow appearance to the piece and leaves a uniform, satin gloss on the surface.

ALCOHOL and SHELLAC are special materials that require proper application. They must be used with great care as they can damage the finish.

ALCOHOL POLISH or SPIRITING is the method of polishing using a pad dipped in alcohol and wrung free of the liquid. The surface of a piece of furniture is wiped with brisk, circular motions until a beautiful luster appears.

FRENCH POLISHING is the application of thin layers of shellac or French varnish to a finished surface with a cloth pad until a high, smooth gloss is obtained.

QUALASOLE POLISHING combines a special material called qualasole with French polishing to produce a long-lasting luster that seems to improve with age.

PAINTING

PAINTING is the covering of the surface with an opaque liquid material. This material produces a uniform-colored surface under which the grain and other characteristics of the wood are hidden. It may be preferable to use paint on a surface if an inferior wood is used, if a more colorful surface is desired, or if the surface is to match another area. Also, paint facilitates cleaning as it is washable and can be cleaned with a mild soap and water without harming the film.

PAINT is a mixture of pigment oil color to give color and body, oil to provide a vehicle in which to disperse the color, drier to accelerate oxidation and shorten the drying time, and thinner to reduce the paint so that it will spread easily ovr the surface.

ENAMEL is a paint or colored varnish that leaves a smooth, hard finish on a surface when it dries. Different types of enamel that produce a glossy, satin-smooth, or dull finish are available.

Paint can be used to create special finishing effects such as antiquing, mottling, and distressing.

ANTIQUING and GLAZING are methods of finishing a new object to make it appear old. Carvings, moldings, and irregular surfaces are emphasized as crevices and corners are darkened to make the elevated portions stand out. Antiquing mellows the surface tones so they are softened yet highlighted. It also covers surface imperfections which might otherwise mar the finish.

MOTTLED FINISHES are two-toned effects in which one shade of color is applied for the background and a contrasting color is applied over it.

DISTRESSED FINISHES are a combination of splattered paint spots, dents, lines, and other marks inflicted by various hard objects on the surfaces of furniture. They imitate the seasoned appearance of old wood and give an illusion of wear and age.

CHAPTER 2   **TEXTILES**

Definition and History of Textiles
Fiber
        Definition of Fiber
        Types of Fiber
          Natural Fibers
          Man-made Fibers
Yarn
        Definition of Yarn
        Fibers and Yarn
Weaving
        Definition and History of Weaving
        Types of Weaves
          Basic Weaves
          Combination Weaves
        Types of Woven Fabric
Knitting
        Definition and History of Knitting
        Knitting Stitches
        Knit Fabric Construction
        Types of Knitted Fabric
Braiding
        Definition of Braiding
        Types of Braided Fabric
Fabric Finishing
        Definition of Finishing
        Types of Finishing
        Dry Finishing
        Wet Finishing
        Special Finishing

TEXTILES

TEXTILE is a generic term referring to both the RAW MATERIALS suitable for making a fabric and the FABRIC itself, which is a cloth made from fibers that have been spun into yarn and then woven, knitted, or braided.

HISTORY OF TEXTILES

Textile production seems to be synonymous with civilization. Archeological excavations as well as writings have produced evidence that textiles were an important commodity in ancient cultures. Carved wooden and clay models, mural paintings, vase decorations, and preserved cloth samples attest to the skill of the craftsmen and the fine quality of the design and texture of their fabrics. The work of making cloth was entirely manual although there was a diversity of methods. Looms were both vertical and horizontal, and weaving was done from the bottom up and from the top down. Yarns were made of cotton, linen, wool, and silk.

Sociological and political aspects color the textile industry. The weavers in ancient Greece formed guilds to protect their rights, and the Romans capitalized on the weaving abilities of the peoples in their empire. A great cloth market rose in the Frankish city of Oddia where King Dagobert decreed that a yearly fair was to be held in honor of the makers of cloth. Trading was heightened among many countries when the Crusaders introduced Near Eastern fabrics to Europe. And the Hundred Years' War counts a textile monopoly agreement between England and France as one of its primary causes.

During the Middle Ages, very stringent laws were passed to govern the textile industries. Weavers were allowed to own two looms, one for narrow cloth and one for broadcloth; and their sole occupation had to be weaving. Only dyers were to color yarns and cloths, and special merchants sold the dyes. Taxes were levied on textile products, and these revenues helped to support governments and to subsidize wars.

To escape these tyrannical rules, weavers fled to other lands. This, along with the rise and fall of various governments and empires, spread the craft around the world. With the migration of the industry's artisans, a great diversity in weaves, designs, and colors developed. Eventually, the need for cloth became so great that manpower was not adequate. Mechanical spinning and weaving devices were devised to ease this burden. The Industrial Revolution continued these technical advances, and the textile industry evolved from a home to a factory enterprise.

Equipment refinement and scientific research have perfected textile products. Man-made fibers are important sources of yarn, and they have necessitated the development of new dyes and fabric finishes. Today, the manufacture of textile products is one of the largest industries in the world. Still, it is interesting to note that the fundamentals — types of weaves and weaving looms — are basically the same; only the methods have changed.

FIBER

FIBER is the fundamental unit of raw material used to produce textiles. It can, by nature, be divided into two groups: natural and man-made.

NATURAL FIBERS

NATURAL FIBER is that fiber which is derived from plant or animal life. It may be cotton, jute, linen, stems, stalks, leaves, bark, grass, silk, or wool.

COTTON is a soft, white, fibrous substance composed of the hairs clothing the seed pods of an erect, shrubby plant of the mallow family. Oriental countries first cultivated cotton about three thousand years ago; and it is believed that India was the first country to grow cotton. The Arabians acquainted Italy with cotton, and the Crusaders introduced it into other European areas. Eventually, it was widely used in all the Mediterranean countries. Thirteenth-century writings first mentioned the English use of cotton, but it was not utilized extensively until the first years of the sixteenth century. The early seventeenth century saw the beginning of cotton cultivation in the United States. With the invention of the spinning frame and the spinning mule in England and the cotton gin in the United States during the Industrial Revolution, cotton production and manufacturing greatly increased. Today, there are cotton fields stretching across the southern United States from Virginia to California.

JUTE is a fibrous skin between the bark and stalk of a plant of the linden family.

LINEN is a long, hairlike fiber that grows in the stalk of the flax plant. Historical records indicate that the first textile fiber used by man was probably linen. Ten thousand years ago, during the Stone Age, Neolithic lake dwellers made fish nets from the flax plant. References to linen are found in many verses of the Bible. The mummies of ancient Egyptian kings and nobles were wrapped in linen cloth after the preservative preparations were completed. The fine quality and durability of these cloths attests to the fact that the arts of spinning and weaving were very advanced.

SILK is the fine, soft, shiny fiber produced by silkworms to form their cocoons. It is the only natural fiber to come in filament form; and it may be either cultivated or wild. Legend surrounds the origin of the silk industry, and two charming Chinese tales envelop its beginnings. The first is about the cocoon that accidentally fell into the teacup of the Princess. She pulled the softened fiber, and it unwound from the cocoon in a continuous strand. The second tells of the Empress Si-Ling-Chi, who produced the first silk fiber so that she could make a robe for her husband. For her efforts, she was known as the "Goddess of the Silkworm." Actually, silk fiber was first spun into cloth by the Chinese about 2600 B.C. The source of the fiber for silk was a closely guarded secret, and silk fabrics were considered a treasure. For hundreds of years they were carried by caravan to the Near East to be traded, and Alexander the Great is said to have introduced silk into Europe during the fourth century B.C. As the fame of the fabulous Chinese silks spread, interest in its production increased. Finally, after three thousand years of secrecy, the origin of the silk fiber and the process for weaving it were discovered and stolen out of China. The people of southwestern Europe eventually developed a large silk industry which continued a westward movement because of the Moslem conquests. In the eighth century, Spain began to make silk products; and during the twelfth century, Italy became so competent with its silk weaving that it was the leader for five hundred years. Finally, France broke this trend and became Italy's rival. Silkworm cultivation has not been commercially successful in the United States. Still, the silk industry is important here because the United States is the greatest importer and consumer of silk.

WOOL is a product of the fleece of sheep or the hair of the goat, llama, alpaca, camel, or vicuna. Originally, wool was a short, fluffy undercoat under the hair on species of wild sheep. Primitive man hunted and killed these sheep to use the meat for food and the pelt for clothing. It is thought that during the first century A.D. ancient shepherds learned to improve the wool by breeding the sheep.

MAN-MADE FIBERS

MAN-MADE FIBER is that fiber which has been produced by a manufacturing process. In 1664, Robert Hooke, the English naturalist, prophesied that man would someday be able to produce artificial fibers.

The French scientist Rene A. Reaumier believed that it was possible to make filaments from gums and resins (1710). Finally, in 1840, an apparatus was invented that would draw synthetic filaments through small holes. Man-made textile fibers were not officially recognized until 1925, when the Federal Trade Commission permitted the use of the term "rayon" for yarns made from cellulose or cellulose derivatives. Again, in 1937, the Commission ruled that the term "rayon" must designate any fiber or yarn produced chemically from cellulose. During the years that followed, many compositions were experimented with until the Commission finally ruled again on February 9, 1952, that there would be two categories of cellulose fibers: rayon and acetate. The Commission further ruled that all fabrics and garments must be labeled to reflect their fiber type and content. Spurred by the success of these man-made fibers, manufacturers employed researchers to investigate other possibilities. Chemists were able to invent fiber-forming substances with particular characteristics, and eventually, fibers made from these substances were marketed. By 1960, confusion had developed because each manufacturer used his own trade name for each of the fibers. To clarify the situation, the United States Congress enacted the Textile Fiber Products Identification Act. In compliance with this Act, the Federal Trade Commission standardized the identification of man-made fibers by assigning them generic names according to their chemical composition. The Commission periodically reviews the terms, adding new ones and deleting or revising as needed. The latest amendment established the following generic names and definitions.

ACRYLIC is a fiber made from a long chain synthetic polymer composed of at least eighty-five percent, by weight, acrylonitrile, a liquid derivative of natural gas and air. Acrylic fibers are a spin-off from Dr. W.H. Carothers's polyester research. Using Dr. Carothers's information as a basis, a large American chemical company developed the first acrylic fiber in 1944. All of the initial efforts were directed toward a product for World War II. After the war, work continued, and in May, 1950, production began on an acrylic fiber. In time, several other chemical companies researched acrylics and developed their own types of fibers. These have been marketed under trade names devised by the manufacturers.

Special characteristics associated with acrylics include dyeability, resiliency, recoverability, cleanability, wearability, resistance to soiling and staining, color retention, and resistance to abrasion. They are nonallergenic and mildew and moth proof.

MODACRYLIC is a modified acrylic composed of thirty-five to eighty-five percent, by weight, acrylonitrile. Experimentation with super-polymers was begun in 1934 by a large American chemical company. It was not until 1949 that the first modified acrylic staple fiber was developed. In July, 1950, commerical production began.

Modacrylic fibers are known for soil resistance, dyeability, resistance to stains, cleanability, color retention, resiliency, recoverability, wear life, fire resistance (self-extinguishing), and resistance to abrasion. They are moth and mildew proof and nonallergenic.

GLASS is a manufactured fiber in which the fiber-forming substance is glass. The fantasy of making yarn and fabric from glass is very old. Renaissance artisans were the first to spin glass strands or rods for decoration on glass objects. During the World's Columbian Exposition, in 1893, Edward Drummond Libbey displayed several articles of woven glass. These articles were composed of glass fibers held together by silk threads, an impractical method of manufacture. Processes for drawing glass fibers were investigated during World War I when Germany experimented with filaments of glass fibers produced from heat-softened glass rods. Then during 1931, the United States perfected this method, and in 1938, two American glass companies merged and began the manufacture of glass textiles. As a result, competitive "fiber glass" production became an important industry after World War II.

NYLON is a thermoplastic polymide resin derived from a coal tar base, air, and water. The discovery of nylon is credited to Dr. Walter H. Carothers and his staff of organic chemists. Dr. Carothers was coordinating a study of polymerization when one of his assistants found that one polymer could be drawn out into a long fiber. Further experimentation proved that one polymide produced an especially good fiber, and a group of engineers and chemists were employed to make it a commercial success. In February, 1935, one polymer was considered better than all the others, and it was named nylon. Nylon was introduced to the public in 1938, and it continues to be produced today.

Nylon is rated as the longest wearing fiber. Its features include dyeability, changeability, resistance to abrasion, stain and soil resistance, ability to recover, resiliency, and color retentiveness. It is moth and mildew proof and nonallergenic.

POLYESTER is a complex ester formed by polymerization. Dr. Walter H. Carothers began the experiments that eventually produced polyesters. When his laboratory decided to concentrate on polymides, some British research chemists pursued polyesters. They studied Carothers's research papers and continued the work, which ultimately produced a polyester fiber. Eventually, companies in the United States took an interest in polyester and purchased the rights to produce and market polyester products. Some companies have continued the research, and today there are several fine types of polyester available.

Polyester is noted for its good abrasion resistance, cleanability, good color retention, ability to accept bright, vivid colors, excellent resiliency, recoverability, stain and soil resistance, and wearability. It is moth and mildew proof and nonallergenic.

ACETATE is a fiber in which the fiber-forming substance is cellulose acetate where not less than ninety-two percent of the hydroxyl groups are acetylated. The term triacetate may also be used. Henri and Camille Dreyfus developed cellulose acetate in England during World War I. It was a nonflammable lacquer to be used on the fabric for the wings and fuselage of aircraft. Continued experiments produced a method for spinning the acetate into fiber filaments. Shortly after this, commerical production began in England, and the United States entered the industry in 1924. With the 1952 ruling of the Federal Trade Commission, acetate became the designated name of the fiber.

ANIDEX is a fiber in which the fiber-forming substance is any long chain synthetic polymer of which at least fifty percent, by weight, contains one or more esters of a monohydric alcohol and acrylic acid.

AZLON is a fiber in which the fiber-forming substance is composed of any regenerated naturally occurring proteins.

METALLIC is a fiber composed of metal, metal-coated plastic, or a core completely covered by metal.

NYTRIL is a fiber containing at least eighty-five percent of a long chain polymer of vinylidene dinitrile content not less than every other unit in the polymer chain.

OLEFIN is a fiber in which the fiber-forming substance is any long chain synthetic polymer composed of at least eighty-five percent, by weight, ethylene, propylene, or other olefin units.

RAYON is a fiber composed of regenerated cellulose. Cellulose nitrate, the first step in the process of making rayon, was discovered in 1855 by George Audemars, a Swiss chemist. Almost thirty years later, in 1884, Count Hilaire de Chardonnet produced the first synthetic textile fibers from nitrocellulose; consequently, he has become known as "the father of rayon." He won the original French patent and with a large financial backing built the first rayon factory.

RUBBER is a fiber in which the fiber-forming substance is comprised of natural or synthetic rubber.

SARAN is a fiber in which the fiber-forming substance is any long chain synthetic polymer composed of at least eighty percent, by weight, vinylidene chloride units. The chemical compound, vinylidene chloride, was an early discovery — 1840. Although the possibilities of its polymerization were known, the intensive research that produced the fiber saran was not begun until 1936. Four years later, in 1940, the fiber was commercialized.

SPANDEX is a fiber in which the fiber-forming substance is composed of a long chain polymer of at least eighty-five percent segmented polyurethane. Until 1930, rubber was the only elastic substance for use in fabrics. It was molded into sheets and cut into narrow strips. A method was developed to extrude liquid rubber into round, fine yarn. Two layers of cotton or rayon yarn were wound around the rubber thread so it could be used in fabric. A stretch yarn, made from nylon filament, was the first elastic yarn made into a textile. The fibers were coiled, curled, or crimped in their manufacture, and their stretch was produced from straightening them. They had good stretch and form-fitting characteristics, but their holding power was poor. Much research has been done to correct this problem. Rubber- and chemical companies·both have been involved in the developmental work of which spandex is the result. This is a highly competitive field, and the specifics of the process are carefully guarded.

VINYL is a fiber in which the fiber-forming substance is any long chain synthetic polymer composed of at least fifty percent, by weight, vinyl alcohol units and in which the total of the vinyl alcohol and any one or more of the various acetal units is at least eighty-five percent, by weight, of the fiber.

VINYON is a manufactured fiber in which the fiber-forming substance is any long chain synthetic polymer composed of at least eighty-five percent, by weight, vinyl chloride units.

NOVOLOID is a manufactured fiber containing at least eighty-five percent, by weight, cross-linked novolac.

ARAMID is a manufactured fiber in which the fiber-forming substance is a long chain synthetic polyamide in which at least eighty-five percent of the amide linkages are attached directly to two aromatic rings.

GENERIC FIBER NAMES WITH CORRESPONDING FIBER TRADEMARKS

GENERIC NAME	TRADEMARK	FIBER TYPE
Acetate	Acele	Filament Yarn
	Ariloft	Filament Yarn
	Avicolor	Solution-Dyed Filament
	Celacloud	Crimped Staple Fiberfill
	Chromspun	Solution-Dyed Filament Yarn
	Estron	Filament Yarn and Cigarette Filter Tow
	Loftura	Slub Voluminized Filament Yarn
	SayFR	Fire-Resistant Filament Acetate
Acrylic	Acrilan	Staple and Tow
	Bi-Loft	Fibers, Filaments
	Creslan	Staple and Tow
	Orlon	Staple and Tow
	Zefran	Acrylic, Dyeable and Producer Colored
	Zefstat	Acrylic
Aramid	Kevlar	Filament
	Nomex	Filament and Staple
Metallic	Lurex	Yarn of Slit Film
	X-Static	Metallic
Modacrylic	Acrilan	Staple and Tow
	Elura	Modacrylic
	SEF	Modacrylic
	Verel	Modacrylic
Nylon	Anso	Nylon Filament and Staple Soil-Resistant Carpet Yarn
	Antron	Nylon
	Beaunit Nylon	Nylon Filament, Staple and Tow, plied and heat set 2500 denier and white and space dyed
	Blue "C"	Nylon
	Cadon	Filament Yarn and Multilobal Monofilament
	Cantrece	Nylon
	Caprolan	Yarns, Monofilaments and Textured Yarns
	Celanese	Nylon
	Cordura	Nylon
	Courtaulds Nylon	Nylon Producer Crimped Filament Yarn
	Crepset	Patented Continuous Monofilament that develops a regular crimp, also available in anti-cling yarn

GENERIC NAME	TRADEMARK	FIBER TYPE
	Enkalure	Multilobal Continuous Filament apparel yarn and textured delayed soiling carpet yarn
	Enkasheer	Continuous Monofilament Torque Yarn
	Monvelle	Biconstituent Nylon-Spandex
	Multisheer	Multifilament Producer-Textured Stretch Yarn
	Qiana	Nylon
	Random-Set	Heat-Set BCF Nylon
	Random-Tone	Fashion and Styling Yarns of BCF Nylon Fiber
	Shareen	Nylon Monofilament Textured Yarn
	Stria	Bulked Nylon Carpet Yarn, Modified Twist
	Super Bulk	Heat-Set, High-Bulk Continuous Filament Nylon Carpet Yarn; Luxurious look of Spun Nylon
	Twix	Bulk Nylon Carpet Yarn, Modified Twist
	Ultron	Nylon
	Variline	Variable Denier Continuous Filament Yarn
	Vecana	Nylon
	X-Static	Nylon
	Zefran	Nylon
	Zefstat	Nylon
Olefin	Herculon	Continuous Multifilament, Bulked Continuous Multifilament, Staple and Tow
	Marvess	Staple, Two and Filament Yarn
	Polyloom	Olefin
	Vectra	Olefin
Polyester	Avlin	Filament Yarn and Staple
	Blue "C"	Polyester
	Caprolan	
	Dacron	Filament Yarn, Staple, Tow and Fiberfill
	Down-To-Earth Tones	Polyester
	Encron	Continuous Filament Yarn, Staple, Fiberfill
	Enka	Filament and Staple
	Fortrel	Filament Yarn, Staple, Tow and Fiberfill
Polyester	Hystron	Polyester
	Kodel	Filament Yarn, Staple, Tow and Fiberfill
	Quintess	Polyester Multifilament Yarns
	Shantura	
	Source	Biconstituent Nylon-Polyester
	Spectran	Polyester
	Textura	Producer Textured Polyester Yarn

GENERIC NAME	TRADEMARK	FIBER TYPE
	Trevira	Polyester
	Twisloc	Polyester
	Vycron	Filament, Staple, Tow and Fiberfill
	Zefran	Polyester
Rayon	Avicolor	Solution-Dyed Filament and Staple
	Avril	High Wet Modulus Staple
	Beau-Grip	Specially Treated Viscose High-Tenacity Yarn
	Briglo	Bright-Luster Continuous Filament Yarn
	Coloray	Solution-Dyed Staple
	Encel	High Wet Modulus Staple
	Englo	Dull-Luster Continuous Filament Yarn
	Enka	Rayon
	Enkrome	Patented Acid-Dyeable Staple and Continuous Filament Yarn
	Fiber 700	High Wet Modulus Staple
	Fibro	Staple
	I.T.	Improved Tenacity Staple
	Jetspun	Solution-Dyed Continuous Filament Yarn
	Kolorbon	Solution-Dyed Staple
	Skyloft	Bulked Continuous Filament Yarn
	Softglo	Semi-Dull Luster Continuous Filament Yarn
	Super White	Optically Brightened Rayon
	Suprenka	Extra-High Tenacity Continuous Filament Industrial Yarn
	Xena	High Wet Modulus Staple
	Zantral	High Wet Modulus Staple
Spandex	Lycra	Spandex
Triacetate	Arnel	Filament Yarn and Staple

YARN

YARN is a group of natural or man-made fibers twisted together to form a continuous strand which can be used for weaving, knitting, or braiding a textile material.

Primitive man invented yarn by interlacing fibers so that they held together and made one long, continuous strand. At first, this was done with the fingers; however, crude hand tools were eventually made. Refinements were added, but the hand tools were used until sometime in the fourteenth century when the "bobbing wheel" was devised. In 1533, a treadle was added to the wheel so that it could be operated by foot, leaving the hands free to manipulate the fiber. Improvements continued slowly until the Industrial Revolution which began the evolution of mechanical spinning. Notable among the devices invented at this time were the parallel rollers (Lewis Paul, 1730); the water-twist frame (Richard Arkwright, 1769), unique in using power other than human to drive it; the spinning jenny (James Hargreaves, 1767), which could spin sixteen threads at once; and the mule (Samuel Crompton, 1779), which combined the best features of all the devices into one machine. Automatic machines have long since replaced these appliances; however, it is interesting to note that the essential features are still being used and that they are the foundation of the industry today.

Fibers are spun into yarn either SINGLY where only one type of fiber is used or in COMBINATION where two or more types of fibers are mixed. Mixtures are successful as complementary fibers are purposely blended to compensate for undesirable qualities.

WEAVING

WEAVING is the process of making a fabric on a loom by interlacing the WARP or lengthwise yarns with the FILLING or crosswise yarns (WEFT).

Primitive man used weaving techniques to produce the few objects he used and needed. For these he chose long fibers that could be woven directly into an article. It was not until later that he learned to twist shorter fibers together to form a yarn. After this achievement, he could use a loom for weaving.

The first looms were very crude and were operated by hand. It is believed that the warp yarns were hung from the limb of a tree with stones tied to the ends to serve as weights. Other looms have been discovered in which the warp yarns were tied between two sticks. A sharpened stick was used to carry the filling yarns over and under the warp yarns. Eventually, a wooden frame was made to hold the warp yarns which were strung in parallel rows. To facilitate the weaving of the fillings, a harness or HEDDLE was devised. It lifted the warp yarns automatically so that the filling could be shot through. Variations of the hand loom were invented and used by the peoples of many civilizations throughout the world; however, it was not until the Industrial Revolution that any attempt was made to run a loom by other than human power. In 1785, Dr. Edmund Cartwright completed a power loom. It was not entirely successful, and over the next thirty years many problems deterred its progress. But continuous technical improvements developed a power loom that began the evolution that became today's vast textile industry.

Weaving consists of three BASIC WEAVES: plain, twill, and satin;

all other weaves, no matter how intricate, are variations of these. Combinations of the different weaves allow the production of many types of fabric surfaces and strengths.

BASIC WEAVES

PLAIN weave is also known as taffeta or tabby. It has one warp over and one warp under the filling throughout the cloth construction. This is the simplest type of construction and, as a consequence, it is inexpensive to produce. It yields a surface that is receptive to direct print.

TWILL has filling threads woven over and under two or more warp yarns, creating diagonal lines on the face of the cloth either to the right, to the left, or to the right and left both. The values of twill are its strength and drapability. It has greater pliability and resilience than plain weave, and it is soil resistant.

SATIN has a smooth, shiny surface caused by floats of warp over the filling or vice versa. Satin weave fabrics drape well because the weave is heavier. Its compactness gives the fabric more body as well as less porosity, which makes the fabric warmer.

Plain Weave

Twill Weave

Satin Weave

COMBINATION WEAVES

BASKET weave has two or more warp ends over and two or more warp ends under in parallel arrangement, interlacing with the filling yarn. It produces an attractive, easily woven fabric that stretches readily and hangs well.

RIB weave is made by cords that run in the warp or filling direction. The corded yarn is covered up by the tight interlacing of the system that shows on the face and back of the cloth.

PIQUÉ also has a corded effect, usually in the warp, but it may have cord in the filling or both ways. Generally, the cords are held in place by a few ends of plain weave construction.

DOUBLE CLOTH, PLYCLOTH, or POCKET weave is two cloths woven together and held in place by binder warp or filling.

BACKED CLOTH weave has one warp and two fillings or two warps and one filling.

PILE weave requires two or more warps and one filling or two or more fillings and one warp. The extra warp or filling yarns make the pile which is looped on the surface of the goods. The pile effect may be cut or uncut on the face, and basic constructions hold the cloth in place. Pile introduces a third dimension creating an effect of depth.

JACQUARD weave produces a cloth reproduction of persons, places, or objects. It uses a special mechanism that allows an unlimited range of intricate designs to be woven. The Frenchman Joseph Marie Jacquard invented a card device so that the warp yarns could be moved independently. The design for a fabric must be drawn onto graph paper. Following this layout, holes corresponding to the design are punched into cards. The cards are laced together and fastened to an apparatus on the loom. As the cards move through the machine, they release the needles that control the heddles. The heddles raise and lower the warp yarns while the filling creates the design. This complicated arrangement may take several weeks to several months to complete, but once it is prepared, weaving is easily accomplished and the pattern can be used and reused.

LENO or DOUP weave has warp yarns that are paired and half-twisted or fully twisted about one another.

LAPPET, SWIVEL, or CLIPSPOT weave has small dots or figures woven or embroidered into the cloth by using an extra filling or warp. These embellishments are placed on a plain weave background.

BATISTE is a fine, sheer, smooth fabric. It is named for Jean Baptiste, a French linen weaver.

BENGALINE is a sturdy, warp-faced fabric with pronounced crosswise ribs formed by bulky, coarse, plied yarn or rubber threads. It originated in Bengal, India.

BIRDSEYE has a small geometric pattern with a center dot resembling a bird's eye. It is woven on a dobby loom with heavier filling yarns that are loosely twisted to make the material more absorbent.

BOUCLÉ is the French word for ringed. The fabric was so named because it has a ring appearance, formed by drawn-out looped yarn on the face of the goods.

BROADCLOTH is a tightly woven plain-weave cloth with a crosswise rib. It was originally a silk shirting fabric, so named because it was woven in widths exceeding the usual twenty-nine inches.

BROADLOOM is carpet woven in widths of six, nine, twelve, fifteen, and eighteen feet.

BROCADE is a rich Jacquard-woven fabric of an all-over interwoven design of raised figures or flowers with the pattern emphasized by contrasting surfaces or colors. The name was derived from the French word meaning to ornament.

BUCKRAM is a ply yarn, scrim fabric with a stiff finish. It was named for Bokhara, in the southwest U.S.S.R., where it was first made.

BURLAP or GUNNY is a plain-weave coarse fabric.

CALICO is a plain, closely woven, inexpensive cloth. It is usually made in solid colors which are discharge or resist printed onto a white or contrasting background. The colors are not always fast. It originated in Calcutta, India, and is one of the oldest cotton staples on the market.

CAMBRIC is soft, white, closely woven cotton fabric calendered on the right side to produce a slight gloss. It was originally made in Cambrai, France.

CANVAS has an even weave that is heavy and firm.

CHALLIS is one of the softest fabrics made. It is very lightweight and usually is printed with a delicate floral pattern. It was named from the Anglo-Indian term, shalee, meaning soft.

CHAMBRAY is a plain-weave fabric with colored warp and white filling that gives a mottled colored surface.

CHENILLE is a fabric woven from chenille yarns and has a fuzzy pile. It is named for the French word meaning caterpillar.

CHIFFON is a thin, diaphanous, or gauzelike, soft, flimsy fabric.

CHINTZ is a glazed cotton fabric often printed with bright figures and large flower designs. Some glazes wash out during laundering, but resin glaze will withstand washing or dry cleaning. It was named from the Hindu word meaning spotted.

CORDUROY is a cut-pile cloth with narrow to wide wales that run in the warp direction of the goods. An extra set of filling yarns make the pile, and the back is plain twill weave.

CREPE is a lightweight fabric characterized by a crinkly surface produced by hard-twist yarns, chemical treatment, weave, or embossing.

DAMASK is a firm, glossy, Jacquard-patterned fabric similar to brocade but flatter and reversible. It was first brought to the Western world by Marco Polo from Damascus, the center of fabric trade between East and West, during the thirteenth century.

DENIM is a rugged, serviceable, staple cotton cloth recognized by a left-hand twill on the surface.

DIMITY is a thin, sheer cloth in which cords or stripes may be woven into the fabric. It is easy to manipulate and launders easily and well.

DOTTED SWISS is a sheer fabric embellished with small dot motifs that may vary in color. It originated in Saint Galen, Switzerland, about 1750.

DUCK is a closely woven, heavy material, the most durable fabric made, according to the textile industry.

FAILLE is a ribbed cloth with crosswise rib effect. It is soft and belongs to the grosgrain family.

FELT is a compact, matted woolen material. The name is derived from the Anglo-Saxon word meaning to filter.

FLANNEL is a fabric with a slight nap on both sides.

FOULARD is a lightweight cloth noted for its soft finish and feel. It is made with plain or twill weaves and is usually printed with small figures on dark or light backgrounds.

FRIEZE is generally made with uncut loops but is sometimes styled by shearing the loops at varying heights.

GABARDINE is a firm, durable, compactly woven cloth which shows a diagonal line on the face of the goods. It is named for a cloak or mantle popular during the Middle Ages.

GINGHAM has dyed yarns introduced at given intervals in both warp and filling to achieve a block or check effect.

GRENADINE is a fine, loosely woven fabric in leno weave.

GROSGRAIN is a heavy, rather prominent, ribbed fabric made from plain or rib weaves.

JASPÉ is a fabric which has a series of faint stripes formed by light, medium, and dark yarn.

LAMÉ is a fabric in which metallic threads or yarns are interspersed throughout or used in the base construction.

LAWN is a light, thin cloth of plain weave with a crisp and crease-resistant finish.

MADRAS is a fine firm cotton cloth with a plain weave background. It is usually striped or plaid in color. Its name was derived from the town of Madras in India.

MARQUISETTE is a lightweight, open-mesh cloth of leno or doup weave.

MATELASSÉ is a soft, double cloth which has a quilted surface effect. It is woven on Jacquard looms.

MELTON is a heavily felted, hard, plain, face-finished cloth. It originated in the famous Melton Mowbray fox-hunting area in Leicestershire, England.

MONK'S CLOTH is made of very coarse yarn and is a rough, substantial, rather bulky fabric with a tendency to sag.

MUSLIN is a generic term for a variety of cotton fabrics.

NAINSOOK is a fine, soft fabric with a plain weave.

NINON is a smooth, transparent, high-textured fabric made in plain or novelty weaves.

ORGANDIE is a very light, thin, stiff, transparent and wiry cloth. Chemical treatment assures that it will retain its crispness through repeated launderings.

OSNABURG is a coarse cloth, often made with part waste in it. It is named for a town in Germany.

OXFORD is a soft, somewhat porous, rather stout fabric with a silklike luster finish.

PANNÉ is named from the French word for plush and is a satin-faced material made with a high luster by a roller-pressure treatment during finishing.

PERCALE is a printed cloth with a smooth, firm finish.

PIQUÉ is a medium weight or heavy fabric with raised cords that run in the warp direction.

PLISSÉ is a fabric treated in a striped motif or in spot formation with a caustic soda solution that shrinks parts of the goods to provide the crinkled or pleated effect.

PLUSH is a warp-pile cloth covered with a surface of cut-pile yarns. The pile is longer but not as densely woven as velvet. Plush is derived from the French term, peluche, by way of the Latin, pilus, which means hair.

PONGEE was originally a thin, natural, tan-colored silk fabric made of wild Chinese silk with a knotty rough weave. It was named from the Chinese, pun-ki, meaning "woven at home on one's own loom." Now, it is also a staple, fine combed fabric finished with a high luster.

POPLIN is identified by a fine rib effect in the filling direction from selvage to selvage.

REP is similar to poplin but has a more distinctive crossrib cord.

SATEEN is made with a satin weave and has a very smooth, lustrous surface effect.

SATIN has a very smooth, lustrous face effect while the back of the material is dull. The name originated in Zaytun, China.

SAXONY was originally a high-grade coating fabric made from the wool of Merino sheep raised in Saxony, Germany. Now, it also is the name for a soft woolen cloth with elaborate yarn effects.

SCRIM is an open mesh, plain-weave cloth in several constructions and weights and usually used in buckram.

SEERSUCKER is a lightweight cloth in which a base warp lies flat and a second warp becomes crinkled because of chemical treatment.

SERGE is one of the oldest basic terms in textiles. It now implies any smooth-faced cloth made with a two-up and two-down twill weave.

SHANTUNG is a silk fabric made of several fibers but designated by an elongated slub filling yarn. It was named for the city of Shantung, China, where it was originally woven.

SHARKSKIN is made from a small twill weave and has a smooth compact surface resembling the skin of a shark.

SHEETING is a plain-weave corded or combed cloth which comes in light, medium, or heavy weights.

STRETCH WOVEN fabrics originated in Germany and Austria and were developed to provide greater freedom of body movement for the athlete. They present very good surface texture and are durable and moisture absorbent. Stretch yarns in the warp of a warp stretch fabric or in both the warp and filling ensure that these fabrics will return to their original shape when tension is released.

SURAH is a soft, twill-woven silk or rayon fabric often made in plaid effects. If made of fiber other than silk, the fiber content must be declared.

SWISS is a fine, sheer, crisp, stiff cloth which may be plain, dotted, or figured.

TAFFETA is a fine, plain-weave fabric, smooth on both sides, usually with a sheen on its surface. It may be solid colored, printed, or woven in such a way that the colors seem changeable. It was named for the Persian fabric taftan.

TARTAN is a cloth made in plain weave or in a two-up and two-down twill weave. This multicolored fabric may be conventional or exceptional when made in variations of color effects. The fabric originated in Spain and was called tiritana, although it is now associated with Scottish clans.

TERRY CLOTH has uncut loops on both sides of the fabric.

TICKING is a compactly woven cotton cloth, usually striped.

TWEED is a rough, irregular, soft and flexible, unfinished, shaggy cloth. It was named for the Tweed River which separates England from Scotland. It is one of the oldest and most popular outerwear fabrics used today. It is made of a twill or a homespun (plain) weave.

VELOUR is a term loosely applied to cut-pile cloths in general. It also designates fabrics with a fine raised finish.

VELVET is a warp-pile cloth in which a succession of rows of short-cut pile stand so close together as to give a uniform, even surface.

VELVETEEN is a filling-pile cloth in which the pile is made by cutting an extra set of filling yarns.

VOILE is a combed yarn, high-twist, staple fabric with a threadlike appearance. The cloth is made from gassed yarns.

ZIBELINE is cloth made from cross-bred yarns, and the fabric is strongly colored. The finish is a highly raised lustrous type, and the nap is long and lies in one direction. The cloth may be given a soft feel and finish.

KNITTING

KNITTING is the art and science of constructing fabric by interlocking yarn loops or stitches with the use of needles.

Early in his history, man invented hand knitting. A pair of heavy, hand-knitted wool socks discovered in an Egyptian tomb and dating from about the fourth century B.C. is the oldest known knitted fabric. Centuries later knitting, or rather the Old English word, cnytton, was found in literature of the year 1492. The fifteenth century saw the perfection of the art of knitting, and within a few generations it had spread throughout Europe.

Originally, needles were carved from bone or wood. These needles generated only coarse meshes and uneven fabric. The Spanish improved this by making steel needles. The first knitting machine was constructed by an Englishman, Reverend William Lee. It produced eight loops to one inch of width, which was too coarse. The Reverend reworked his machine so that it could knit twenty loops to one inch. Modern knitting machines still use the principles of Reverend Lee's machine, but the average number of loops is now twenty-eight.

KNITTING STITCHES

Knitting consists of vertical rows of stitches called WALES and horizontal rows of stitches called COURSES. Some common knitting stitches are plain, rib, tuck, and purl.

PLAIN STITCHES produce a smooth-faced material; they are used in making fine, thin, or sheer fabrics.

RIB STITCHES produce lines of wales on both sides of the fabric causing the fabric to be very elastic.

TUCK STITCHES are formed by holding one loop on a needle while taking on one or more additional loops and then casting all of them onto another needle.

PURL STITCHES have successive courses of stitches drawn to opposite sides of the fabric, thereby making it very elastic in the lengthwise direction and quite elastic in the crosswise direction.

The interlocking loop gives knitted fabrics some unusual characteristics. Foremost is the ability to stretch in any direction, thereby giving good fit without binding. Second, knit construction contains insulative air pockets that give warmth, yet the material is porous and allows the air to be pushed through. These fabrics are also lightweight, wrinklefree, and very absorbent. Some undesirable qualities can be produced from a loop as well. Certain knit fabrics tend to sag and lose their shape or they may shrink. Others run easily, and none are windproof. But remedial measures have been devised to counteract some of these deficiencies and others are still undergoing testing.

KNIT FABRIC CONSTRUCTION

Knit fabric construction includes circular knit, rib knit, flat outerwear knit, and flat underwear knit.

CIRCULAR KNIT is made on a circular machine and produces a tubular fabric without seams.

RIBBED fabric is made with two sets of needles to give a ribbed or corrugated surface to the fabric.

FLAT OUTERWEAR fabric is made by having the needles arranged in a straight line.

FLAT UNDERWEAR fabric is made on a machine with only one set of needles.

TYPES OF KNITTED FABRIC

DOUBLE KNIT is a fabric knitted with a double stitch on a double needle frame to provide a double thickness that is the same on both sides. This type of fabric has excellent body and stability.

INTERLOCK KNIT is a special type of eight-lock knit cloth that has a smooth surface on both sides.

JERSEY is a plain-stitch knitted fabric.

KNIT PILE is a fabric produced by sliver knitting, a method of knitting both yarn and fiber into a fabric to provide an exceptionally deep pile effect.

MILANESE KNITTED fabric is known for its high gauge, lightweight, fine texture, and appeal in hand. The warps always move in the opposite direction with the full threading or color arrangement to produce a run-proof fabric.

PLATED is a knit fabric that has one kind of yarn on the face while another type is found on the back of the goods.

RACHEL KNIT fabric is a versatile fabric that can be made from every type of yarn of any type of fiber in any form.

SINGLE KNIT is a fabric knitted on a single-needle machine. It has less body, substance, and stability than double knit.

TRICOT is a type of warp-knitted fabric that has a thin texture since it is made from very fine yarn. It is taken from the French verb tricoter, which means to knit.

VELOUR is a popular knit fabric with properties that are similar to woven velour.

BRAIDING

BRAIDING is the interweaving or intertwining of three or more strands of yarn or other material so that the strands pass over and under one another. Braid construction may be geared to produce flat, narrow tapes or strips as well as center-cored rounds or hollow tubes. The resulting material is especially suitable for shaped articles. Notable among these textiles are the STRAWS, fabrics made by braiding natural plant fibers. Some of the straw materials are Baku, Balibuntal, Leghorn, Milan, Panama, and Tuscan.

BAKU is a fine, lightweight, expensive straw with a dull finish.

BALIBUNTAL is a fine, lightweight, glossy straw obtained from unopened palm leaf stems.

LEGHORN is a fine, braided straw, made from a special wheat grown in Tuscany, that has been cut, bleached, and worked by hand.

MILAN is a fine, closely braided straw.

PANAMA is fine, handbraided, creamy colored Toquilla straw made primarily in Ecuador.

TUSCAN is fine yellow straw woven from the tops of bleached wheat stalks grown in Tuscany.

FABRIC FINISHING

FINISHING is the art and science of applying desired surface effects to fabrics.

No matter what its color, cloth taken directly from the loom after its manufacture, is called "gray goods." The "gray goods" is taken to the perch where it is inspected and blemishes are marked so they can be remedied by the finishing. The material is then subjected to the finishing processes and converted from "gray goods" to the finished fabric. There are many types of finishes because they must be adapted to the types of fibers used and to the intended purpose of the fabric. Generally, finishes are divided into two categories: dry and wet.

DRY FINISHING

DRY finishes are those processes in which the goods are handled in a dry condition. These finishes include burling, specking, calendering, glazing, napping, shearing, gassing or singeing, and scheinerizing.

BURLING is the removal of loose threads and knots from woolens by means of a tweezer type tool called a burling iron.

SPECKING is the removal of specks, burrs, and other detrimental objects that might impair the final appearance of woolens.

CALENDERING is an ironing process that adds sheen to a fabric by passing the cloth between sets of rollers mounted on vertical frames. Many finished effects can be produced by using combinations of heat, pressure, various types and numbers of rollers, and surface friction.

GLAZING is the application of starch and glues to cloth followed by friction calenderizing to give fabrics luster, sheen, polish, or shine.

NAPPING is the brushing of fabrics to cause surface fuzziness. The fibers are raised by means of teasels (dried flower heads) or rollers covered with one-inch-high steel wires. Napping makes cloth more compact and durable, softer and smoother; thus, it provides warmth.

SHEARING is the trimming of the pile on pile fabrics to give them an attractive smooth surface.

GASSING or SINGEING is the burning off of any protruding fibers by passing the cloth over a gas flame or heated copper plates. This is an essential process for fabrics that are to be printed because a smooth surface is required.

SCHEINERIZING is a method of milling in which a roller made of steel and engraved with many fine lines pounds and flattens the threads in the cloth and imprints very fine ridges that reflect the rays of light and bring out the surface characteristics by which the fabric is known.

WET FINISHING

WET finishes are the chemical operations that are used to finish cloth. Wet finish processes are soaping, fulling, scouring, mercerizing, souring, dyeing, and printing.

SOAPING is the treatment of cloth with a soap solution prior to fulling.

FULLING is the application of heat, moisture, soap, and pressure, followed by a cold rinse, to cloth in order to shrink it and give it a more compact body.

SCOURING is the cleaning of a cloth or its surface by washing and an abrasion or rubbing treatment.

MERCERIZING, a process discovered accidentally by John Mercer in 1844, consists of impregnating cloth with a strong, cold, caustic soda solution to increase the affinity for dyes and the luster of the surface.

SOURING is the neutralizing of any alkali content in the fabric by treating the cloth with a weak acid solution.

DYEING and PRINTING are finishing processes that give beauty to a fabric through the addition of color and design and pattern.

DYEING is the immersion of the fiber, yarn, or fabric in the dyestuff solution in order to saturate the fabric with color.

Dyes have been used by man since primitive times to beautify cloth. Originally, dyes were obtained from plant, animal, and mineral sources; however, in 1856, the first synthetic dyes were derived from coal tar. Until World War I the United States imported these synthetic dyes. As the supply of imported dyes was terminated then, the United States built its own industry which, today, is unsurpassed.

Good dyes are expected to provide durable color and this indicates that certain properties should be present. Dyes must be COLOR-FAST and keep their original color without bleaching or FADING in the light and without running or BLEEDING when laundered. They must also be WEAR-FAST which means that the color will not rub off or CROCK. To ensure that these characteristics hold true, the dye itself must be properly matched to the fiber, and the dye method must be compatible with the fiber, yarn, or fabric. Some of the major dyeing procedures are bale, batik, beam, burl, chain, cross, jig, package, piece, random, raw stock, resist, solution, stock, top, union, vat, and yarn.

BALE DYEING is a process in which the material is sent, without finishing, through a cold water bath where the sized warp yarns have an affinity for the dye. The filling yarn will not absorb the dye as the natural wax has not been removed.

BATIK DYEING, which originated in Java, is one of the oldest forms known to man. Designs are created by coating sections of the cloth with wax; the dye is absorbed only by those portions that are unwaxed.

BEAM DYEING saturates warp yarn wound on a perforated beam with color by forcing the dye through the perforations.

BURL or SPECK DYEING is a hand operation in which the colored specks or blemishes in a cloth are covered with colored inks.

CHAIN DYEING involves tacking cloths of low tensile strength together end-to-end and then running them in a continuous chain through a dye bath.

CROSS DYEING produces varied color effects from a single dye bath by using fibers with varying affinities for the particular dye used.

JIG DYEING uses rollers to pull the fabric through a deep dye bath in a jig, vat, or beck as many times as are needed to achieve the desired shade.

PACKAGE DYEING colors the yarns while they are on the cones.

PIECE DYEING provides a solid, single color for a cut or bolt of fabric.

RANDOM DYEING tints only certain designated portions of the yarn.

RAW STOCK DYEING dyes the fiber prior to its being spun into yarn.

RESIST DYEING requires a prior treatment of the yarn or cloth so that only those portions not treated will accept the dye.

SOLUTION DYEING adds the color pigment to the solution in which the filaments of man-made fibers are being formed. This method produces colors that are bright, clear, clean, and fast.

STOCK DYEING means that the fibers are dyed after they have been degreased and dried, but before they are spun into yarn.

TOP DYEING circulates dye through top wool ropes that have been wound on perforated spools.

UNION DYEING is the coloring of two or more different fibers in the same dye bath to produce different shades of the same color.

VAT DYEING designates that the cloth has been dyed through the use of vat dyes.

YARN DYEING indicates that the yarn has been dyed prior to the weaving of the goods.

PRINTING involves imprinting a pattern or design on the fabric in one or more colors using dyes in paste form.

Techniques used for printing include application, block, blotch, burn-out, direct, discharge or extract, duplex, overprinting, photographic, print-on-print, resist, screen or stencil, shadow, stipple, vigoreux, and warp.

APPLICATION PRINTING is actually a direct printing method in which white goods of any type is printed upon.

BLOCK PRINTING is the oldest form of printing known to man. It is a tedious hand operation in which motifs are cut into wooden, copper, or linoleum blocks, one for each color to be used. The color is applied to the block and then the fabric is stamped.

BLOTCH PRINTING is a direct printing method in which the ground or base effect is colored as well as the design area.

BURN-OUT PRINTING produces a raised motif on a sheer ground. This is made by printing a motif with a chemical that will burn out one of the types of fiber yarns.

DIRECT PRINTING prints motifs directly onto bleached fabric as it passes over color rollers etched with designs. There is one roller for each color to be used, and it is etched only with that portion of the design related to the particular color.

DISCHARGE or EXTRACT PRINTING produces a dark fabric with a white motif by bleaching out certain areas and then direct printing over them to give the finished effect.

DUPLEX PRINTING is the printing of both sides of the goods with the same or different motifs.

OVERPRINTING superimposes colors or motifs over colors already on the goods.

PHOTOGRAPHIC PRINTING transfers photographic prints to fabric by the use of photo-engraved rollers.

PRINT-ON-PRINT is a method of printing used to achieve special effects. Each color has its own roller, an essential to providing a clean, clear print.

RESIST PRINTING uses a tannin-mordant paste to cover the fabric. The areas to be used for the motif are stripped, leaving them white. Then the fabric is piece-dyed to color all the white areas.

SCREEN or STENCIL PRINTING uses a screen spread over a frame. The design is copied onto the screen, and portions of it are covered with glue. The fabric is placed under the screen and dye is pushed across it by a squeegee. The covered areas will not allow the dye to pass to the fabric. A different frame must be used for each color and for each part of the design.

SHADOW PRINTING produces a mottled effect by using a printed warp and a white filling when the fabric is woven.

STIPPLE PRINTING adds small dotted effects in spaces and bare areas of a printed motif.

VIGOREUX PRINTING is another name for TOP dyeing.

WARP PRINTING uses a warp yarn that has been printed on a beam and rewound onto another beam at the back of the loom. It is then woven with a white or light-colored filling to produce a mottled effect in the fabric.

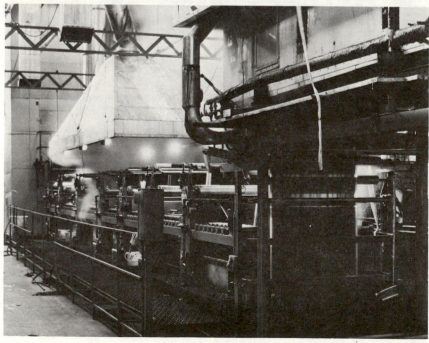

SPECIAL FINISHING

Besides the finishes that enhance the appearance of a fabric, there are special processes that increase its serviceability and durability. These treatments prolong the life of a fabric by protecting the surface so that the fiber can resist wear more easily.

SHAPE RETENTIVE finishes provide a fabric with the ability to retain its shape.

WRINKLE RESISTANT finishes prevent creasing of a fabric by unintentional folds or rumples.

WASH AND WEAR finishes or DRIP-DRY finishes allow a fabric to dry smooth after washing so that it will need little or no ironing.

PERMANENT PRESS finishes give a fabric the ability to retain a certain shape. With this finish, the fabric is treated, the piece is sewed, then it is cured or set.

WATER REPELLENCY is a finish that resists the absorption or penetration of water for a given period of time.

WATERPROOF finishes completely seal the fabric in a substance insoluble in water.

ABSORBENT finishes increase the absorbency of any fabric.

FLAME PROOFING finishes *retard* a fabric's burning or flaming activity but do not make it entirely fireproof.

MOTH PROOFING is a finishing applied to wool fabrics by impregnating the yarns with a chemical.

MILDEW PROOFING is a chemical finish that retards the growth of mildew fungus.

ANTIBACTERIAL finishes impart a self-sterilizing quality to a fabric.

SLIP-RESISTANCE finishes give permanent firmness to fabrics. The cloth is immersed in synthetic resins and stretched and dried under tension.

HEAT-REFLECTANT finishes are insulation treatments for fabrics. The cloth is treated with a metallic substance; then when the fabric is sewn, the metallic side is faced toward the area where heat is to be kept in or away from the area where the heat is not wanted.

FOAM LAMINATING is an insulating finish. By trapping air in cellular pockets in the foam and then adhering the foam layers to a fabric, a good, lightweight insulating material is produced.

FABRIC-TO-FABRIC BONDING is a finish in which a permanent bond is effected between two fabrics. It produces a self-lined fabric that retains its shape better, and it gives stability to knitted fabrics.

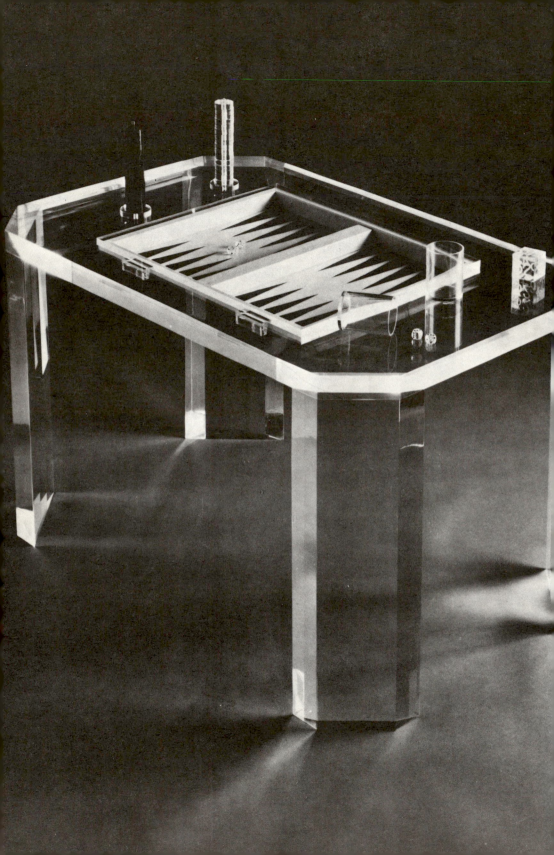

CHAPTER 3   **PLASTICS**

Definition of Plastic
Groups of Plastics
        Thermosetting
        Thermoplastic
Methods of Fabrication
        Casting and Molding
        Forming
Coloring
Construction
        Polishing
        Fastening
Plastic Materials
        Laminate
        Resin Board

PLASTICS

PLASTIC is a generic term for chemically produced resinous materials. It is a man-made substance consisting of a great number of diversified ingredients that may be wholly or partly combinations of carbon with oxygen, hydrogen, nitrogen, and other organic and inorganic polymers that have very long chains of repeating units derived from short molecules. When these chains are heated, they move apart and slide over one another, yet they retain their cohesiveness.

GROUPS OF PLASTICS

The chief characteristic of plastic is that it will soften when it is heated, but it will not melt. This allows heated plastic to be shaped by the application of mechanical stress. When it has cooled, the plastic will remain in the desired shape after the stress is removed. Plastics are divided into two groups: thermosetting and thermoplastic.

THERMOSETTING

THERMOSETTING designates plastics that are set in a *permanent* shape by heat and pressure and that will *not* soften if they are reheated. They include polyurethane, polyester, and melamine.

POLYURETHANE is a synthetic rubber polymer.

POLYESTER is a polymer resin formed chiefly by condensing polyhydric alcohols with dibasic acids.

MELAMINE is a synthetic resin made by condensing formaldehyde with melamine, an amonium thiocyanate distillate.

THERMOPLASTIC

THERMOPLASTIC refers to plastics that will soften when they are heated and that will harden when they are cooled, no matter how many times the process is repeated. Some of these plastics are acrylic, polypropylene, and polystyrene.

ACRYLIC is a colorless, pungent acid that is formed into a resin by polymerizing its esters.

POLYPROPYLENE is a very light, highly resistant resin made from polymerized propylene, a colorless gas obtained in the refining of petroleum.

POLYSTYRENE is a tough, clear, colorless plastic, the result of the polymerization of styrene.

METHODS OF FABRICATION

The basis for the fabrication or shaping process of plastics lies in their ability to slide into new positions when they are heated and to remain in these positions when they are cooled. These processes are divided into two methods: casting or molding and forming.

CASTING AND MOLDING

Casting and molding require that the plastic material be *fluid:* either in a hot, molten state or as a liquid at or about room temperature.

LIQUID CASTING uses syrupy or liquid plastic resins that are poured into molds and are cured by heating or by chemical reaction. Casting produces sheets, rods, and special shapes.

LOW-PRESSURE MOLDING is used to shape plastic that has to be reinforced. The liquid resins are mixed with mats or fibers of such materials as glass or asbestos, and the resulting substance is molded at a low pressure.

SLUSH AND ROTATIONAL MOLDING uses plastisols and plastigels which are combinations of resins and other ingredients in paste or liquid form or in a gel. The plastic is put into a mold and left to set until a layer is formed on the surface of the mold. When the desired thickness is reached, the unsolidified plastic is poured off, and the layer is left to finish hardening.

INJECTION MOLDING is a method for shaping plastic in which the plastic is fed from a hopper into a heating chamber where it is softened to a fluid state. The plastic fluid is pushed at high pressure through a nozzle at the end of the chamber into a cool, closed mold. Here the plastic cools and becomes a solid shape. Then the mold is opened and the finished item is ejected. Injection molding is the principal process for forming thermoplastic materials.

COMPRESSION MOLDING is a technique for producing shaped plastic in which the resin granules or powders are placed in an open mold and are subjected to heat and pressure after the mold is closed. This converts the plastic to a liquid, and as it cools it becomes a solid, finished form. This method is commonly used for thermosetting plastics.

TRANSFER MOLDING is a type of compression molding. The resin is heated in one chamber and then transferred by force into the cavity of a heated closed mold.

FORMING

Forming is the fabrication of a plastic that is in a *solid* state.

SHEET FORMING is used to shape thermoplastic materials. A sheet of plastic is heated above the temperature of its softening point. It is placed over a mold and shaped by the application of pressure from mechanical or hydraulic force, from preheated compressed air, or from vacuum techniques.

EXTRUSION is a process in which the softened plastic is forced through a die to produce rods, tubing, and cross-sectional shapes in long lengths. It may be used with most thermoplastic and some thermosetting plastics.

POWDER MOLDING involves the fusing of plastic powder under heat and pressure until it takes on the shape of the surface of a mold.

COLORING

Plastics lack color when they are manufactured; however, an enormous range of colors can be produced through the addition of dyes and pigments. They are generally added during the chemical processing so that the color becomes an integral part of the plastic material. The property of plastic that allows it to accept color is an important feature as plastic can be made to match any color scheme or resemble wood grains and tones and hard surface substances such as tile, stone, or brick.

CONSTRUCTION

Plastic is a rigid, solid material, and as such it can be machined. However, heat builds up from the friction of the moving tool so precautions must be taken to prevent the heat from softening the plastic material or causing it to change shape. This problem is generally solved by cooling the plastic with streams of cold water as it is being worked.

POLISHING

Plastic shapes must be polished after fabrication. Often surfaces and edges need to be refined, especially if they are to be exposed. Sometimes spurs or notches must be removed and the disfigured patch smoothed into the surrounding area. All this is accomplished both manually and mechanically with mild abrasives and water. Finishers wearing white gloves may polish a surface with a soft pad that has been soaked in water and dipped into a grinding powder. Automatic machines with rotating tables and buffers covered in suedelike material can be set to rub flat-surfaced pieces. As the plastic revolves under the circling buffer, it is sprinkled with water and a polishing agent and ground to a fine surface luster.

FASTENING

Fastening of the plastic shapes and components together may be accomplished with a conventional method: that is, bolts or screws may be pushed through holes drilled in the plastic and secured to another piece. However, the preferred procedures are those that utilize the special properties of the plastic itself.

The first of these is the refrigeration/warming process. The readied plastic is put into a refrigerated unit and cooled overnight to forty degrees. As the plastic cools, it *shrinks*. When it is removed from the chamber, it is cut to size and fitted into its designated pocket. As the plastic returns to room temperature, it *expands* to its original measurements, and the union becomes tight.

Joinery also takes advantage of the traits of the plastic material. To form a proper joint, the edges of both pieces must be straight and flat. After they are fitted, they are coated with an adhesive. This is a resin epoxy that acts as a catalyst between the pieces being joined and causes a chemical reaction so that both sides melt and fuse. The edges must be worked together carefully to eliminate any air bubbles that might have formed. The weight of the pieces will hold them together until the epoxy has hardened. Once the pieces are firmly affixed, a saw is run across the joint to remove any excess resin. Then the joint is polished so there is a little ridge or indentation to catch the light and reflect it.

PLASTIC LAMINATE

Another type of plastic substance can be created by laminating. LAMINATING is the building of a surface material by bonding two or more thin sheets or layers together. The core may be several thicknesses of craft paper soaked with phenolic resins and covered by a melamine resin, or it may be wood chips mixed with resin. A middle layer of materials saturated with plastic may be used. The veneer is usually melamine resin in various colors, designs, or photographically reproduced natural wood grain. The layers are cemented with a contact adhesive and are placed in a large hydraulic press between stainless steel plates. They are then subjected to pressure and extremely high heat to form a hard-surfaced sheet. Finally, the surface is polished into a gloss, satin, textured, brushed, or furniture finish.

PLASTIC RESIN BOARD

A substance that can be used effectively for surface material in furniture construction is RESIN BOARD. It is produced by floating a liquid resin over a structural stock. It is usally made with a polyester resin that has been treated. A flexibility agent is added to increase the "give"; and it is conditioned with a flame retardant. The foundation is either one-half or three-quarters of an inch thick and may be plywood, flakeboard, or particle board. An item can be any color as the resin can be tinted to a desired shade; it can be as large or as small in size as is needed; and a truly rectilinear shape with all the sides parallel can be obtained. It is a sound, strong, and firm material whose understructure bears the stress of the form, and it will withstand a great deal of abuse.

PART II

CHAPTER 4 — **WALL COVERINGS**
CHAPTER 5 — **FLOOR COVERINGS: CARPETS AND RUGS**
CHAPTER 6 — **WINDOW COVERINGS: DRAPERIES AND CURTAINS**
                                   SHADES
                                   BLINDS
                                   WOVEN SHADES
                                   SHUTTERS

CHAPTER 4   **WALL COVERINGS**

Definition and History of Wall Coverings
Color and Design
Wall Covering Surfaces
      Plain
      Printed
Types of Wall Coverings
      Wallpaper
      Plastic (Vinyl)
      Metal (Foil, Mylar)
      Textures
            Grass Cloth
            Flock
            Cork
            Burlap
      Textiles
Sizes of Wall Coverings
Lining
Adhesives
Quantity of Covering
Installation

WALL COVERINGS

WALL COVERING is a comprehensive term used to designate the substances that are applied to the surfaces of walls and ceilings.

HISTORY OF WALL COVERINGS

Although paper was invented by the Chinese about 105 A.D., the other peoples of the world were slow to learn the process. In fact, paper-making was not introduced into England, on the other side of the world, until 1490. The English made progress quickly and, about nineteen years later, produced papers designated for use on walls. One of the earliest creators of wallpaper was Hugo Goes. Fragments of a paper he designed have been found at Cambridge University and were scientifically dated at the year 1509. The French became involved with wallpaper about one hundred years later when a group known as Les Dominotiers developed a unique, highly figured design. Their style was called Domino as were their papers.

Early English and French wallpapers were hand stenciled or painted. Artists were commissioned by wealthy clients to decorate sheets approximately thirty by twenty-one inches that were fitted together to make a complete pattern. A few of these printed papers still survive in England. Other decorative techniques used during this period were block or letterpress printing and flocking. Some examples of this flocking can be found, but the oldest piece is from Worcester and has been dated about 1680.

Painted Chinese papers, generally known as India Papers, were contemporary with the flocking. They were developed especially for European trade and began to appear there in the latter part of the seventeenth century. They were distinctive because each sheet was unique, thus rendering each length free of repetition. Lengths of original Chinese papers have been preserved and are on display in Nostell Abbey, Yorkshire, England, and Woburn Abbey, Bedfordshire, England. These highly prized papers were copied by European artisans using etched plates or wood blocks to produce the design and stencil or brush to apply the color.

The migration of the Eckhardt brothers from Holland to England in the late 1700s brought an innovation to English papers. The Eckhardts devised a method for applying silver to papers so that it would resemble lace or damask fabric. Patterns now could have two levels of luster with bright and dull surfaces adjoining.

Popular interest in wallpapers was extensive. It had become an accepted substitute for wood panelling, leather, tapestry, and printed cloth, and it was admired for its clever and inexpensive simulation of the other materials. Its inherent possibilities soon became evident, and it became a medium in its own right. Fresh designs in stripes, chintz patterns, and geometrics were produced.

It became necessary to increase the production of wallpaper and technical advances made this possible. Around 1785, Christophe-Phillippe Oberkamph constructed the first wallpaper printing machine. To complement this invention, a process for manufacturing endless rolls of paper was designed by Louis Robert. Machine printing did not appear in England until 1840 when a printing company in Lancashire introduced the method.

Although the age of mass-produced wallpapers was imminent, hand printing continued to flourish. The supremacy of French design and execution peaked at the beginning of the nineteenth century. This was the era of flocked paper, the distemper-colored papers of Jean-Baptiste Reveillon, and the panoramic decorations by Joseph Dufour. Similarly, English papers reached an apex, but this was not until the middle of the century. The foremost English paper designer was William Morris. His style, which first appeared in 1862, was notable for its flat, naturalistic patterns and rich, subdued colors. Another innovator was Walter Crane, whose progressive designs were contemporary with those of William Morris and with the traditional work in the Rococo and Gothic styles of A.W.N. Pugin, Owen Jones, and James Huntington.

Wallpaper development reached a hiatus after this and for the next one hundred years, no outstanding advances were made. Interest in wallpapers as an art form was revived in the 1950s and 1960s, and wallpapers became accepted as a primary tool for interior design. Improvements in designs, manufacturing, and materials furnished a variety of coverings ranging in style from the original traditional to the latest visual arts.

The United States followed the French and English trends and imported wall papers from these countries during the eighteenth century. Patterns resembling marble, small Domino patterns, and other designs were shipped over in large quantities. Finally, a wallpaper business was begun by the firm of John Howell and Son in Albany, New York, with John Rugar also of New York and John Bright of Boston. Not much of their work has survived, but some of it can be seen on bandboxes or in trunks where it was used as lining. There was a definite preference for scenic papers commemorating the American Revolution, and other designs have been discovered in eighteenth and nineteenth century mansions that have been restored.

A decline in wallpaper use and manufacture followed, but the development of silk screen printing and the influence of the European Art movements revived an interest in wallpaper as an art form. The American hand-screen firms developed non-traditional designs which were highly successful and gave impetus to the use of wall covering for interior design.

COLOR AND DESIGN

Wall covering is an attractive alternative to paint. Like paint, it brings color into a room, but it can bring pattern as well. The numerous wall covering patterns may be grouped into categories for identification purposes. These categories are floral, modern medallion and simulated ceramics, geometric, antique textile, conversation piece, texture, trellis and grille, children's, and period.

FLORAL patterns are one of the most favored of all wall covering designs as they are reminders of nature's gifts of flowers, fresh air, and sunshine. Like real flowers, they are represented individually or in bunches and are available in every size. They are not restricted to one category but are incorporated into other design styles as well.

MODERN MEDALLION and SIMULATED CERAMIC patterns display a design confined within an outline.

GEOMETRIC patterns combine lines and curves into abstract figures that may be bold, strong, large, or small, including plaids, checks, and dots.

ANTIQUE TEXTILE patterns borrow details from antique cloths such as damask, paisley, or toile.

CONVERSATION PIECE patterns are covering designs that portray a scene, usually with figures in motion. This can be anything from an old-fashioned street scene to a famous opera to a woodland.

TEXTURE patterns have a three-dimensional surface effect.

TRELLIS and GRILLE patterns copy the common objects they portray, and they are often adorned with vines, flowers, or other objects from nature.

CHILDREN'S patterns are those having a juvenile appeal such as clowns, letters and numbers, animals, or storybook people and scenes.

PERIOD patterns copy the designs of wall coverings from various historical eras. Significant styles are Renaissance, Baroque, Rococo, Louis XVI, Directoire, Regency, Empire, Georgian, American Colonial, and French Provincial.

RENAISSANCE designs embrace the "rebirth" of classical forms, and they are a combination of realism and accuracy, good form, and pictorial balance.

BAROQUE designs are characterized by freedom, a manifest reaction against the cold and formal Renaissance. Although they maintain the classical balance, they boast extravagance, grandiosity, and richness, and reflect the prosperous period in which they were originally used.

ROCOCO designs are light in style and in their time witnessed a return to nature with flowers, leaves, stems, and bamboo as prominent features. An important branch of the Rococo was Chinoiserie, a style derived from Chinese decor.

LOUIS XVI designs are a blend of classicism and romanticism featuring straight lines and symmetry with slender proportions and lightened and grayed colors.

DIRECTOIRE designs revert to classicism, and wall coverings are plain and striped, with motifs from agriculture — ploughs, scythes, and wheat.

ENGLISH REGENCY designs reflect the French Directoire; however, the simplified styles are based on Greek classical forms and the honeysuckle plant.

EMPIRE designs are largely derived from fabrics and imitate draped or plaited materials or costumed figures, but Napoleonic events, Greek and Roman architecture, and landscapes are also important.

GEORGIAN designs revive Renaissance styles with balanced and elegant prints that are often marked off by striped borders. Large countryside scenes and urns of flowers are among the patterns that develop the formal atmosphere.

AMERICAN COLONIAL and FRENCH PROVINCIAL designs reflect the native arts and crafts of both countries.

WALL COVERING SURFACES

Wall covering is classified according to its surface type. PLAIN wall covering is usually of a solid color with a flat or textured surface. Textured surfaces are difficult to color and must be given special handling. They acquire their surface designs from fibers supported on a backing of paper or cloth. The fibers are colored by dyeing, but they respond unevenly to the dyes and the color gradually darkens or lightens across a strip. Abrupt changes of color may be avoided if the strips are alternately reversed when they are hung so that every other strip is hung upside down.

PRINTED wall covering has a stamped surface design of one or more colors that creates an overall pattern or mural. These designs fall into two categories — machine prints and hand prints — depending upon the manufacturing process employed.

MACHINE PRINTS are mass-produced in "runs" on high-speed printing presses. A RUN is the strip of covering which can be up to several thousand feet long, that is realized from a single dye batch. Many matching rolls are cut from this strip, and each roll is labeled with a run or lot number so it can be identified later. Numbering is necessary as prior or subsequent dye lots may be of a slightly different color.

HAND PRINTS are made with the stencil process of silk screening. Each roll is individually screened so there are variations in the color from roll to roll. This can be handled by distributing the strips on the walls so that the shading changes are less noticeable.

Designs are laid out on the covering so that the pattern will straight-match or drop-match.

STRAIGHT-MATCH DESIGNS stretch across the full width of a strip, and sections of the same design are on both the left and right edges of the paper. The pattern repeats *horizontally* across each strip when the pieces are matched.

DROP-MATCH DESIGNS repeat *diagonally* across a strip. The pattern extends beyond the width of a single strip, and it is drawn so that the last section of a pattern at the bottom of a strip matches the first section of the same pattern at the top of the adjacent strip.

CUSTOM wall covering designs can be created for a particular job. They may be original patterns or special compositions of stock materials in which the ground, screens, or colors have been assembled by choice. Most shops have a minimum order for custom coverings ranging from six to twenty-one rolls. Besides the charge for the paper, there is a set-up fee to cover the preparation of the screens. This makes the entire operation quite costly; therefore, it may be economically feasible to specify custom wall coverings only with large contract jobs where many rolls are required.

TYPES OF WALL COVERINGS

Wall coverings are currently available in a number of materials: paper, plastic, metal, and textiles.

WALLPAPER is a decorative and practical covering for walls and it is made from long sheets of paper. This paper must be of a quality stock that will accept pigments as the surface is usually painted, stenciled, or printed with abstract, ornamental, or narrative designs.

PLASTIC COVERING is made from a vinyl sheet that has been laminated to a backing and then painted, screened, or printed with ornamental patterns on the face. The vinyl is a strong, manipulatable material that is available in a range of gauges from thick to thin. The backing may be either paper or cloth depending on the surface treatment. Paper backing gives better printing results for both hand- and machine-printed vinyls, while cloth backing permits various textured effects to be worked into the face.

METAL COVERING is manufactured by laminating aluminum foil to a cloth or paper backing. The surface may be decorated with hand- or machine-printing, painting, or screening with equal success on either type of backing.

Synthetic metal covering is made from MYLAR, a polyester film that has had a metallic coating laid on its surface. Printing, stenciling, or painting may be applied over the coating if figured covering is required. This produces the same effect as a foil, but the quality is softer. The film is backed with paper or cloth to give it stability and to facilitate hanging.

TEXTURES are wall coverings with special surface effects that are, or seem to be, three dimensional. Usually, the face is a rough material that casts shadows in the natural or artificial light of an area giving the interesting depth appearance. The items used to create this element are natural or processed materials, applied decorations, and synthetics that duplicate original materials. Textures include grass cloth, flocks, cork, and burlap.

GRASS CLOTH is an Oriental wall covering made from the honeysuckle vine. The stalks are sun-dried and pulped; then the fibers are woven into cloth. As this is a natural material, color and shading are not uniform, but a synthetic version made of cellulose can fulfill this requirement. Both the natural and the synthetic products are backed with paper, although there is also a foil-backed variation that gives a mellow metallic base.

FLOCK was originally fine powdered wool when the art of flocking first appeared during the Middle Ages. Surfaces treated with glue or still tacky with drying paint were spread with the flock. It was allowed to set and then the residue was blown or brushed off. This technique was first applied to paper in the seventeenth century. "Velvet paper" was created by painting, stenciling, or printing a design on the paper with a slow-drying adhesive or varnish and then covering this with the flock. "Counterfeit flock" was paper on which powdered color had been sprinkled instead of flock. In 1634, a patent for flocking was awarded to Jerome Lanyer.

Today, flocks are wall coverings that have a design made of finely ground particles that have been deposited on an adhesive until a gentle profile is built up. They are produced by machine as well as hand printing processes, and they may have paper, vinyl, or foil backgrounds. Flocking and its companion adhesive come in many colors that complement or contrast with the covering on which they are applied. It resembles a pile surface on a fabric and has a velvety feel.

CORK is adhered to paper to produce unusual wall coverings. Printed, raised patterns are formed by laying cork dust on a white ground and then hand-screening colored designs over it. Thin cork wafers glued onto colored coverings—usually red, orange, or black—constitute all-over, embossed, geometric textures.

BURLAP is a wall covering devised from ordinary hemp or jute sack cloth. It has a slightly fuzzy face that provides an effective texture in both plain and printed styles. Most burlap has a paper backing to stabilize the mesh and to simplify hanging.

TEXTILE wall covering consists of ordinary or specially prepared woven fabric.

Historically, textile wall coverings date back in time several centuries and are actually the oldest type of wall covering. They were used during the Middle Ages to keep out cold and drafts in rooms where heating consisted mainly of fireplaces. This was true for churches as well as homes, and there are still pieces of painted textile draperies hanging in twelfth- and thirteenth-century churches. These pieces did not adhere directly to the walls but were loosely hung so they could be easily moved. Eventually, they became permanent fixtures, and from the late seventeenth through the eighteenth century they were mounted in frames and fastened to the wall. Paper wall pictures and then patterned wall paper began to substitute for textiles, and as it is considerably less expensive, it has become the more popular medium.

Fabrics make beautiful, if expensive, wall coverings. They allow a limitless choice of designs as well as the option of matching a pattern in the upholstery goods being used in a room. Some solid color fabrics in plain or textured weaves are painted, screened, or printed to highlight the texture or to supply a desired style.

Almost any fabric produced can be used as a wall covering. Special handling may be required in the application, but it can usually be satisfactorily adhered to most surfaces. Many fabrics are made ready for hanging when they are manufactured by laminating them to a paper backing. These are fastened to the wall by the traditional methods.

Walls may also be upholstered with fabric. They are first lined with wood strips and filled with padding of sheet wadding or flannel to give body, fullness, and stability to the surface. The fabric panels are seamed together to produce a wall-size section with a matched pattern. This is basted to the wood strips and then stretched to fit. It is permanently fastened with tacks, staples, or velcro tape. The edges are trimmed evenly and finished along the ceiling line and baseboard with gimp or self-welt.

SIZES OF WALLCOVERINGS

A SINGLE ROLL is the established unit of measurement for wall coverings. It may be from fifteen to fifty-four inches wide and, when combined with the length, should contain approximately thirty-six square feet of covering material. This will allow at least thirty square feet of usable covering as a certain amount of waste from trimming is inevitable.

Many manufacturers and hangers have found that it is preferable to have the strips cut into double-, triple- and quadruple-length rolls called BOLTS. The advantage in this extra length is that a greater number of floor-to-ceiling strips can be realized with a minimal amount of waste.

LINING

LINING is an inexpensive blank stock or white paper, in widths of twenty to twenty-seven inches, that is applied to the areas that are to be hung with wall covering. It provides a smooth surface and covers many irregularities, even on rough walls. It also serves as an absorbent ground, much like a blotter, that will receive most types of paste and will create a better bond between the wall and the covering. It is absolutely essential that lining be used under certain papers, such as foils that must have a smooth surface for reflective purposes, or types that tend to pull away from their backings when wetted with an adhesive.

ADHESIVES

ADHESIVES are the bonding agents that fasten the coverings to the walls. The durability of the job rests with the adhesive; unless it is compatible with the wall-covering material, the life expectancy of the job will be quite short. Because it is such an important factor in the success of a job and because such a wide variety of adhesives is necessary to hang the many different kinds of coverings, manufacturers insert an information sheet in each roll. This sheet specifies the recommended adhesive type, the installation directions, and the inspection stipulation; plus any additional information that may be necessary.

Wallpaper can be successfully hung with most inexpensive pastes, but a wheat paste is the most common type used.

Plastic is a difficult material to adhere to a wall surface. It requires careful handling to keep the seams from separating and the edges from curling. Also, it does not breathe and mildew readily forms behind it. To combat these problems, special vinyl adhesives have been developed from chemicals, quick-drying elements, and mildew preventatives.

Metal (foil or Mylar) coverings are generally applied with vinyl adhesive although those with a cloth back may also be fastened with wheat paste.

Textures can be pasted up with a wheat mixture or a stainless cellulose paste. If they have been vinylized or have a metallic background, vinyl adhesive should be used.

Textiles are manufactured from such a variety of fibers and backings that the bonding agent must be selected carefully. Either wheat or stainless cellulose paste or vinyl adhesives can be used depending on the covering material.

Some types of coverings are available PREPASTED, that is with dry adhesive already on the back. This greatly simplifies the hanging procedure as the covering only requires moistening to make it ready to be put on the wall.

QUANTITY OF COVERING

To estimate the amount of wall covering necessary for a room, the perimeter (the running feet around the walls) should be measured. This figure is multiplied by the height of the wall (baseboard to ceiling or dado to ceiling.) That amount is divided by thirty to give the number of single roll units. For every two openings (doors and windows), one roll may be subtracted. If the design has a repeat, about twenty percent should be added to the estimate figure or approximately one roll for every five rolls.

Covering for a ceiling is determined from the area of the floor plus any dormer, bay window, cutback, or extension areas. The total figure is divided by thirty to find the number of single rolls needed.

To ensure correct wall covering orders, every designer should be able to ESTIMATE the amount of covering required for a job. However, it must be emphasized that, for ordering purposes, the hanger should be responsible for MEASURING the job.

INSTALLATION

Wall covering is best applied by a professional paper hanger who will have the training and experience to do the job efficiently and correctly. As some of the special types of coverings require particular skills and knowledge, it is preferable to hire someone who has previously worked with that covering. The most appropriate method for obtaining a hanger is through referrals from other designers. A referral implies that a job was satisfactorily completed and that the craftsmanship and reliability of the hanger were acceptable. If an unknown installer must be hired, it is good procedure to request to see some examples of his work and to inquire if the client was pleased with the result.

Included in the hanger's responsibilties for the job are MEASURING the area to be covered to determine the number of rolls required; INSPECTING each roll *before* it is cut as replacement will be made by the manufacturer if a flawed roll is returned uncut; and HANGING the covering. It is also customary for the installer to cover all electrical outlet and switch plates. In addition, he supplies his own equipment and any necessary adhesives.

CHAPTER 5   **FLOOR COVERINGS: CARPETS AND RUGS**

Definition and History of Carpets and Rugs
Fibers
Color
Carpet and Rug Construction
Methods of Manufacturing
      Weaving
         Wilton
         Axminster
         Velvet
         Chenille
      Knitting
      Tufting
Backing
Cushion
Installation
Oriental Rugs (Antique)
American Orientals

CARPET is a thick, heavy fabric made especially as a floor covering. It is produced in long rolls of specified widths by weaving, knitting, or tufting natural or man-made fibers. It is generally sold by the square yard and is installed wall-to-wall to cover the entire floor.

RUG is a single piece of compact, woven, knitted, or tufted fabric intended as a floor covering. It is manufactured of natural or man-made fibers and is produced in various lengths and widths as well as a number of shapes — round, square, oval, or rectangular. Each rug is a separate unit and is meant to cover only a portion of the floor area. Therefore, rugs are usually sold individually.

HISTORY OF CARPETS AND RUGS

The production of rugs began when early man used natural materials — sand, grass, pine needles — to cover the floors of his dwellings. He learned to spread clumps of sheep wool on the hard-packed earthen floors and then to tread them into feltlike rugs. He also interlaced strips of soft wood bark, plant fibers, or animal skins to form mats. Finally, with the advent of spinning, he was able to produce textile rugs.

Rugs were flat-surfaced weaves initially, but as the art evolved, technical advancements allowed intricate designs to be woven. The resulting patterned weaves were called TAPESTRY after the ancient word for carpets, TAPIS. Actually, the first tapestries were rugs with a thick, heavy texture. Their designs were very simple and they had only a few colors. To produce shading, cross-hatching at right angles to the weave was done.

The ancient Syrians were among the earliest tapestry weavers, and it is thought that they introduced the art to the Egyptians. Weaving has had a long history in Egypt. Drawings of looms date from 3000 B.C., and actual tapestry remnants have been found, dating from 1448 B.C. to 1420 B.C. The Egyptians are credited with the refinement of tapestry weaving techniques. Some of the most famous tapestry weavers were the Copts, early Egyptian Christians, whose unique designs and patterns were known in many areas. From the year A.D. 200 through A.D. 1000, their superiority was unquestioned, and much of their work was exported, especially to the Mohammedans.

Tapestry weaving spread northward into Europe when the Romans sent Coptic weavers to Gaul to teach weaving. France began a tapestry weaving industry, but it was not until some Spanish Moors settled at Aubusson in the Creuse Valley that rug weaving was refined. Under the tutelage of the Moors, the French weavers developed tapestry rug making to perfection. The beautiful Aubusson rug is a testimonial to this fact. Mid-European countries became involved in tapestry weaving with Bessarabia, Yugoslavia, Poland, and Italy producing tapestries of extraordinary loveliness. In Norway and Sweden, unique tapestry rugs were designed to adhere to the national characteristics of simplicity and functional beauty.

The art of tapestry weaving was known in the Western Hemisphere prior to the arrival of the Spanish. Indians in Peru and Bolivia produced beautiful tapestry, some of which has been recovered from ancient burial sites. The Pueblo Indians from the southwestern United States also wove tapestry, and it was from the Pueblo that the Navajo learned the craft. Early Navajo weaving was simple and consisted mainly of blankets; however, as their expertise grew so did quality, design, and style, and in 1890, the first rugs appeared.

Developing in tandem with tapestry were pile-weave rugs. The Babylonians were the earliest weavers of these rugs, and Babylon is the site of the first rug industry. When the Babylonians were conquered by Persia, the Persians acquired the skill. They developed the art of rug making and invented the knot called SEHNA which is the root of pile weaving. These rugs became world famous as a consequence of their being traded in the international markets. Related knots were devised by other civilizations — the GHIORDES in Turkey, the SPANISH, and the RYA in Scandinavia — and hand-tied rugs became an important commodity, causing the industry to flourish.

The art of pile rug weaving was brought to Europe when the Moors invaded Spain. It spread across the continent where features unique to each area developed as can be seen in the deep pile rugs of Austria, the handsomely dyed rugs of Germany, the Savonneries of France, and the Scandinavian Rya and Flossa rugs. England became involved when the returning Crusaders introduced the technique. From this knowledge they evolved their own rug types — the Wilton and the Axminster.

Rug making underwent a complete revolution when mechanical devices were attached to the looms. They made the work easier but changed the characteristics of the rugs. Previously, each rug was unique; mechanization made them uniform, both in design and workmanship. As the Industrial Revolution gained momentum, hand-tied methods were replaced almost entirely by power looms.

England was largely responsible for promoting these advancements as farsighted industrialists set up factories in the leading weaving centers. The city of Kidderminster began the machine weaving industry with flat-surfaced ingrain carpets which were among the earliest rugs to be woven by these methods. The Earl of Pembroke established a factory

at Wilton that used Brussels looms to produce pile-surfaced rugs. Eventually, Brussels loom factories were opened in Moorfields, Axminster, and Kidderminster.

Continued innovations enhanced the growth of the industry. In 1825, a new loom was created by combining the principles of the Jacquard and the Brussels looms. Richard Whytock devised a method for predying yarns with patterns and made possible the mechanized weaving of tapestry and velvet rugs. The method for weaving chenille rugs was invented in 1839 by William Quigley and James Templeton.

The rug weaving industry was introduced into the United States by W. P. Sprague in 1791. He imported looms from Europe and built a factory in Philadelphia to produce Axminster rugs. In 1839, Erastus B. Bigelow constructed the first power rug loom. It wove an ingrain type of carpet, but in 1848 he perfected a power loom to produce Brussels weave carpets. Halcyon Skinner invented moquette, a type of spool weaving for making Axminster rugs.

Not only did weaving methods change but the mechanics of the loom improved. The first looms were water powered, but later the power source became electricity. The size of the loom was also subjected to a drastic change. At first, the loom could produce only narrow strips of carpet twenty-seven inches wide. But in the early 1920s, "broad looms" that could weave seamless carpeting nine feet across were constructed. This led to twelve-foot widths in the 1930s and fifteen-foot widths in the 1940s. Today, power looms have been perfected so that unlimited varieties can be produced, and the manufacturing of rugs and carpets has become a complex and exacting process.

FIBERS

Both natural and man-made fibers are used for the production of rugs and carpets. Among the fibers preferred are wool, rayon, acetate, nylon, polyester, acrylic, and grasses. These may be used singly or in combinations and blends depending upon the desired result. Generally, they are selected for their dyeability, durability, and cleanability.

COLOR

The mill purchases yarn by the pound in the natural state so it can dye the yarn to its own specifications. This allows an endless variety of colorations. Generally, the mill subscribes to a scheme of colors that makes up a standard list; however, it is also possible to order custom colors.

Manufacturers' preferences vary concerning their plans for dyeing. Some companies dye the yarn before it is converted into rugs and carpet-

ing. Yarn that is predyed can more easily absorb the color, and the color is beautiful, long-lasting, and quite permanent. Inventories of the dyed yarn may be stockpiled, or the yarn may be dyed piecemeal as it is needed. Other companies dye or print on the piece after it has been fabricated. Various methods, including vat dyeing, resist dyeing, and tack dyeing, are used depending on the particular specifications and requirements.

Many mills have the facilities to dye, while others prefer to job out the process to a service that specializes in this area. Dyeing is a critical operation, and the permanence of a carpet's beauty depends largely on the control of the dyeing process. Fibers, yarns, dyes, processing chemicals, and finishing products must be subjected to exacting tests by skilled chemists before the dyeing procedure can be initiated. Dye chemicals are matched to fibers and the colors are mixed by technicians who check them regularly to determine their constancy. This is especially important because each fiber or yarn shipment is different even though it may have been produced in the same way, and this may cause a variance in the dye affinity. Some companies have installed computer systems to substantiate tests and to mix colors, thereby ensuring color fidelity.

The DRYING phase of the dyeing or printing process is also a critical operation as the drying determines the finish. While the carpet is in the drying oven, the moisture content must be continually checked to ensure that the piece is drying at a constant temperature and rate. If the carpet is too wet, the pile will crush and the backing may remain sticky. If it is too dry, scorching may result, and the backing may become too stiff.

CARPET AND RUG CONSTRUCTION

The construction of a rug or carpet determines its surface appearance. Most rugs and carpets have a pile surface. PILE is the soft, velvety, raised surface produced by making yarn loops on the body of the material. The pile may be finished in several ways: cut, uncut, combination, or sculptured.

CUT PILE is produced by shearing the loops and untwisting the yarn to achieve a plush effect.

UNCUT PILE retains the yarn loops for a pebbly, harder texture.

COMBINATION CUT AND UNCUT PILE uses both types of pile finishes to create interesting textures and appealing patterns.

SCULPTURED PILE is produced by fastening the yarn loops at different heights so that patterns may be formed.

A few types of rugs and carpets are manufactured with a flat surface. FLAT designates a rug or carpet *without pile* that has the same surface texture on both sides and that is reversible.

Several methods are used to manufacture these surface effects; among them are weaving, knitting, and tufting.

WEAVING

Woven rugs and carpets are produced by intertwining the surface pile and the backing simultaneously into an integrated whole. The standard weaves used by the rug and carpet manufacturers are Wilton, Axminster, velvet, and chenille.

WILTON weave is named for the weave developed in the town of Wilton, England, where a factory employing French weavers was established in 1740. Eventually, the Jacquard loom was adapted to weave these rugs so that elaborate patterns with five or six colors could be produced. In Wilton weaves, only one color at a time is drawn into the pile on the surface; the others are buried in the body of the carpet. The strength and resilience which result from this method of weaving give the carpet added quality. The loom can be set to produce a desired pile height, and the pile may be cut, looped, or both.

AXMINSTER weave is named for the small town in southwest England where it was first made on hand looms. The power loom to produce it was invented by an American, but the name has remained unchanged. It is a very sophisticated loom that weaves by drawing pile yarns from large spools of colored yarns. The spools are set in predetermined sequences so that the yarn will be pulled into the loom's weaving section at the right moment to be worked into the design. The weave created is characterized by an even pile height, a heavily ribbed back, and a many-colored pattern whose variations are limitless.

VELVET is the simplest carpet weave, and it is well suited for plush or velvet finishes in solid colors. Variations in color are possible through the use of multiple-stranded and colored yarns or by modifying the loom. The weaving mechanism may also be altered to produce various types of pile surfaces or textures such as loop or plush, mixed pile heights, or a combination of these with cut and uncut pile.

CHENILLE rug making originated in Glasgow, Scotland, and the processes were patented there in 1839. Chenille is the most expensive rug-weaving method as two loom operations are required. The chenille fur or blanket is woven and then cut into strips to make the filling for the second loom. A dense pile that has a wide range of designs, colors, widths, and depths results.

KNITTING

Knitting machines were first adapted to carpet manufacture in the 1950s. Rugs are knitted on machines using three sets of needles that loop the backing, stitching, and pile yarns together in a single operation. The pile surface can be single level or multilevel and is left uncut. Knitted carpets are usually solid colors or tweeds, although pattern and texture variations have recently been made possible through mechanical innovations.

TUFTING

Tufting is the most recent development in the manufacture of carpeting. Actually, the technique of tufting is quite old, as it was first developed by early settlers in the southeastern United States. They saved the wick ends trimmed from homemade candles and used them to create pile in their fabrics. This process was not widely known or used, although, in the 1930s, some machinery was built to produce tufted fabric. In the 1950s, tufting became a significant method for manufacturing rugs and

Wilton Weave

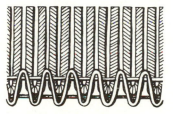
Axminster Weave

Tufting

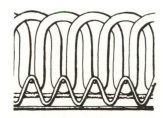
Knitting

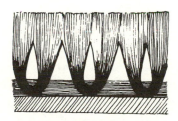
Tufting Fuse-bonded

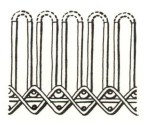
Velvet Weave

carpets as advanced engineering technology made possible the development of the complicated tufting machines. The loom has a bar penetrated with thousands of needles stretching across its width. Yarns are threaded through these needles, and the needles are forced into a prewoven backing material. The yarn is fastened into the backing and when the needles are raised, tufts or loops are made. To prevent the tufts from slipping out of the backing, a coating of latex is rolled over it. Tufting makes possible many types of patterns and designs in both solid and variegated colors as well as cut, uncut, or sculptured piles, and combinations of these.

A variation of the tufting process inserts the pile yarn directly into the liquid vinyl plastisol and then fuse-bonds these components together. Fuse-bonding produces a carpet with a continuous impermeable vinyl back and a cut-pile face. This is the method used in the manufacture of indoor/outdoor carpeting.

BACKING

For a long time the carpet face was the major concern of the manufacturer; however, today, great importance is also attached to the backing. With reference to carpets and rugs, backing has two definitions.

BACKING is the stiff, close, firmly woven underside of the carpet or rug. It is usually made of jute, cotton, or kraftcord, a tough yarn made from wood pulp. It is the foundation of the carpet or rug and supports the pile. For woven and knitted rugs, the backing is formed as the rug is created. Tufted rugs, however, require a prewoven backing into which the tufts can be fastened.

BACKING is also a layer of material affixed to the underside of the carpet. Originally, jute was used almost exclusively, but in 1964 man-made carpet backs in both woven and unwoven form were introduced. A later innovation was the cushion back which comes in five basic types: embossed pattern latex, sponge rubber, solid and foam type vinyl, polyurethane foam, and high-density foam.

The material for the second backing is chosen to complement that used in the construction of the carpet. This ensures uniform stretching or shrinking and reduces the tendency of the carpeting and the backing to separate. These second backings improve the dimensional stability of the rug or carpet, add weight to make it lie flat, and reduce stretching when it is laid. They help prevent rotting and mildewing as they are bonded to the rug or carpet with a clear, natural rubber latex which completely seals it.

If additional backing is required for tufted carpeting or rugs, it is pressed onto the wet latex backing where it readily adheres to the sticky substance. Special materials, including knitted acetate fibers or woven or knitted paper cloth, are used in this procedure.

CUSHION

CUSHIONING is a pad or lining placed under a carpet. Originally, no lining was used under a rug. Then, for a short time, heavy paper was placed under rugs to protect the hardwood floors. In the 1920s, a foreman in a plant producing felt products for industrial uses put some of the felt under the carpet in his office to prevent heat loss. The felt fulfilled its promise and insulated the office, but it had no permanence, as it was too soft. Company engineers capitalized on the idea and developed a durable carpet cushion. At first, a plain, all-jute lining was manufactured, but it was not widely accepted. Refinements resulted in waffle lining (1924) which was immediately adopted by hotels and theaters because of its resilience and luxurious texture. This was the humble beginning of the carpet cushion market. Other companies entered the field, and today, carpet cushion manufacturing is a large enterprise.

Carpet cushion, by federal ruling, is required to be a felt sheet of hair, felt roll hair, cellulose rubber, rubber-coated jute, or animal hair. Its selection should be considered in relation to the height and weight of the carpet pile and to the amount of traffic through an area, as padding lengthens the life of a carpet by absorbing the shock of movement over the pile. In addition, it preserves and protects the backing fibers, reduces the noise level, and diminishes heat loss while helping to provide a more comfortable walking surface.

INSTALLATION

Only a professional installer should be hired to lay carpeting. A reference from a design colleague is the most satisfactory means by which to obtain an experienced, reliable installer. He and the designer should work together to determine the job specifications and to plan the installation. There are many architectural problems in each individual environment which need special attention; therefore, it is important to know what type of installation would be most suitable. Also, careful planning can save money, time, and labor while producing a more aesthetic result.

Samples of each carpet type in all the desired colors plus an example of the underlay cushion and the installation accessories should be examined and discussed. Layout drawings following the actual floor plan and indicating the spaces to be covered should be produced. These drawings can then be used to determine the necessary width for the carpeting. This is essential as the carpet width should equal the maximum width of a room to limit the number of seams. The drawings should also show the locations of the seams. Seams should not be perpendicular to doorways or entries, and seams occurring parallel to a doorway should be centered directly under the door. Seams falling at the change of direction in a corridor should follow the wall line parallel to the carpet direction. Cross seams required because of odd roll lengths should be placed so that they avoid conspicuous locations — doorways or pivot points. By mapping out the seam placement, piecing can be limited to a minimum number of sections, wear can be minimized, and good appearance can be assured.

Once the dimensions of the area to be covered have been established, the installer can figure the number of square yards of carpeting and undercushion needed for the job. It is the designer's responsibility to order the carpet from the mill, and he should request that each bundle be clearly marked as to size, dye lot, and fiber content.

Prior to installation, the floor should be inspected so that repair work can be done and the floors can be cleaned and dried. Also, doors that swing over the carpeted area must be trimmed to give sufficient clearance.

Cushion material is laid in the longest possible lengths with a minimum number of sections. The sections should be placed so that the seams do not coincide with those of the carpet. Cushion laid over wood floors is stapled or tacked in just enough places to keep it from shifting. Padding laid over concrete is cemented to the floor with an approved adhesive. Rubber padding should be installed to allow for a slight stretch.

Carpet lengths are stretched drum-tight along both the length and the width, the pile on all strips running in the same direction. Seams may be *sewn* with waxed linen thread or *sealed* with tape that provides both pins and adhesive. The carpet is held to the floor by several methods, all of which involve tacking.

The most common method for installing carpet is on tackless stripping. TACKLESS STRIPPING is a narrow piece of wood with rows of angled pins protruding from it. It is secured permanently to the floor by nails, adhesive, or double-faced tape with the pins pointing toward the wall. The carpet is gripped securely by the pins which are hooked into the backing.

Another procedure involves turning and tacking the carpet. The edge of the carpeting is turned under one and one-half inches and then

94

tacked down alongside the wall molding.

Sometimes the carpet is installed by tacking it flush with the baseboard and then covering the tacks with quarter-round molding to conceal the edges and to give a finished look.

The carpet may also be laid out in the room, stretched, and stay-tacked about two feet back from the wall. It is trimmed to make it the exact size required, folded back to the stay-tacks and bound along all the edges. It is finish-tacked tight against the wall molding, and the stay-tacks are removed.

It may be necessary for the installer to return to a job site to re-stretch the carpeting. He may also be recalled to fasten a loose edge or to repair a pulled seam. These services are usually included in the first year's guarantee, but thereafter they are performed only for a fee.

ORIENTAL RUGS (ANTIQUE)

Oriental rugs are works of art. They are remarkable for their deep pile, close weave, fine yarns, subtle patterns, rich colors, and fast dyes. They were woven on vertical looms and the pile was created with silk or wool yarns that were *knotted by hand* and cut with a knife at the desired length. The pattern was worked through on both sides and straight, braided, or knotted fringe was formed by extending the warp threads.

Designs and colors vary according to the region of origin. PER-SIAN rugs, named KASHAN, HAMODAN, KIRMAN, or SARUK after the towns where the designs were first made, have predominantly floral patterns with occasional human or animal figures. TURKISH rugs, called BERGOMA, LADIK, GHIORDES, KOULA, and MILAS, generally have a simple geometric design with a longer pile and a coarser construction. CAUCASIAN rugs, identified by the names KABISTAN, SHIRVAN, KAZAK, and KARAJA, are small in size and have geometrical designs with sharp outlines in combinations of red, blue, and yellow. TURKOMAN, desig-nated BOKHARA, BESHIR, TEKKE, TURKOMAN, and SAMARKAND, are characterized by a distinctive center field design of rows of octagonal medallions in red, white, brown, and green and by wide-webbed pileless ends. BALUCHISTAN or BALUCH rugs are very similar to the Turkoman with ends of wide webbing and vivid red and brown colors.

The weavers in India developed three types of rugs which are categorized as Oriental. HAND-TIED rugs come from the District of La-hore, Punjab Province. NUMDAHS are small rugs made of felted goat hair that are hand embroidered with ''tree-of-life,'' floral, or vinelike patterns. DRUGGETS are rugs of simple and colorful designs made from the fleece

of white-haired sheep or a mixture of this fleece and cow hair in a jute backing.

CHINESE ORIENTAL RUGS have a rich, deep pile with designs concentrated on circles of flowers and dragons in colors that are predominantly blue or tan.

Oriental rug weavers expressed their artistic and poetic feelings through the designs and shapes they created for their rugs. These designs and shapes eventually came to designate the rug for a specific purpose.

PRAYER RUGS, carried by the followers of the Moslem religion, were spread on the ground and knelt on during prayer. They have a niche at one end which was placed in the direction of Mecca.

HEARTH RUGS, with niches at both ends, were family prayer rugs.

MOSQUE or MECCA RUGS, for which the rug makers created their most exquisite designs and produced their finest workmanship, were used as prayer rugs in mosques.

DOWRY or WEDDING RUGS were woven by a girl as she grew up, and became part of her dowry when she married.

GRAVE RUGS bore the symbol of mourning, the cypress tree, and covered the body before burial and the grave after interment.

SADDLE BAGS or pouches fastened together by webbing were used to transport cargo on camels.

RUNNERS were long rug strips used as couch coverings.

SAMPLE CORNERS were two-foot-square sections of rug used to display the quality of the weaving to a potential buyer.

FLOOR COVERINGS were room-size rugs, scatter rugs, or mats.

AMERICAN ORIENTALS

American Orientals are machine-made rugs that resemble hand-tied Oriental rugs in design and color. They can be woven with Wilton, Axminster, or velvet construction. Some have the pattern woven through the backing as do the hand-tied Orientals, while others have an ordinary backing. They are given luster by washing with a chemical solution.

CHAPTER 6   WINDOW COVERINGS: DRAPERIES AND CURTAINS

Definition and History of Draperies and Curtains

Styles of Window Coverings

      Draperies

      Curtains

      Valances

      Tiebacks

Hardware

      Rods

      Brackets

      Hooks

      Holdbacks

      Weights

Construction

      Dimensions

      Fabric

      Linings

      Interlining

      Headings

        Pleats

        Scallops

        Shirring

Installation

Workrooms

WINDOW COVERINGS: DRAPERIES AND CURTAINS

DRAPERIES and CURTAINS are fabric window coverings arranged to hang in soft or tailored folds.

HISTORY OF WINDOW COVERINGS

Draperies and curtains have a long and varied history. Prior to the Christian Era, they were used in the Orient to cover windows and doors. Carvings and drawings authenticate their existence, and historical records of commerce verify their use, as they were important articles of trade. Other literary works mention wall hangings in temples and palaces. Southern European civilizations incorporated draperies into their life styles primarily as wall decorations or doorway coverings.

A long period followed in which draperies were not widely utilized. During the Dark Ages, men lived by fighting and life was unsettled. Windows were merely observation slits and had to be readily accessible, while furniture was collapsible and easy to move. Draperies were used as aids to heat retention, however, and churches and castles were decorated and made more comfortable by them. This situation changed in the Middle Ages as the warring subsided. Windows began to increase in size; still, it was not essential to cover them as they were too small to cause problems of light control and privacy. Heating continued to be a troublesome area, and arras, tapestry curtains, were hung over the stone walls in the homes of the rich, and counterfeit arras of painted or stained linen were used in simpler dwellings to alleviate the cold. Warm sleeping rooms were created by curtains that were hung from the ceiling around the huge wooden beds.

Plain thin curtains hanging in vertical folds began to appear at the large glazed windows of the Renaissance period, and occasionally, velvet, damask, or brocade draperies were used. As castles evolved into palaces and textile output increased, wall hangings and bed curtains became very elaborate; in fact, some rooms were completely festooned with wall hangings. During the Rococo period, less emphasis was placed on hangings. Draperies were seldom used on the walls and bed curtains were scaled down in size or were only hung at the head of the bed. The window was the focal point, and curtains, often of two or more layers of different materials, were hung from decorative rods with ornamental ends. Sometimes they were covered by a cornice board or a valance with ruffles, pleats, swags, or jabots.

In contrast to this, draperies and curtains were designed along more simple, tailored lines in the years that followed. But, in the Victorian era, they again were sumptuous and ornate. Thick brocades and velvets trimmed with fringes and braid were hung over undercurtains usually made of lace. The twentieth century has favored functionalism, with draperies and curtains being used for the more practical purpose of solving window covering problems. Less formal materials in styles that include pleated headings and the extended curtain which covers an entire wall are the preferred treatments.

STYLES OF WINDOW COVERINGS

Windows are covered with fabric to enhance an environment through color and design. But more importantly, textile window treatments ensure privacy, regulate and filter light, insulate against both heat and cold, and absorb sound.

DRAPERIES are panels of fabric that have been sewn together and hung *at the windows*. They are usually made from fabric that is medium-to-heavy in weight and they may be lined or unlined. LINED draperies have a double thickness consisting of outer panels of the drapery fabric itself and backing panels of a less expensive material. UNLINED draperies are single panels of the drapery fabric that are sewn together and finished.

Draperies may be hung so that they are stationary at the side of the window and serve only a decorative purpose, or they may act as a covering that can be opened or closed at will. Generally, they open in the center and pull back to both sides — TWO-WAY DRAW — an appropriate plan for most types of windows. Draperies may also be set up to pull in only one direction — ONE-WAY DRAW — to either side. Such an arrangement is best suited for corner windows, bay windows, and walls of glass with a door opening or a short wall on one side.

Styles are designed from single- and double-rod treatments. A SINGLE-ROD treatment involves a traverse or decorative rod with one layer of drapery that is usually lined or of a heavy fabric. A DOUBLE-HUNG treatment has two rods and two sets of draperies: OVER-DRAPERIES that are lined or of a heavy fabric and UNDERDRAPERIES of a lightweight or sheer fabric. In the double-hung styles, both sets of draperies may draw, only the overdraperies may open, or the over-draperies may be tied back while the underdraperies draw.

Balloon-tied Over Drapery with Under Shade

Swag Bell Valance on Pole with Drapery

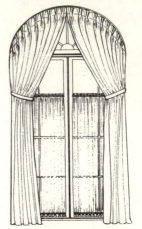

French Pleats with Shaped Top and Under Curtain

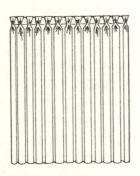

Plain Butterfly Pleated Heading

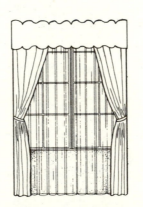

Shaped Cornice with Self Tieback Over Drapery and Under Curtain

Shirred Over Drapery with Under Curtain

Shirred Curtain with Sunburst and Rosette

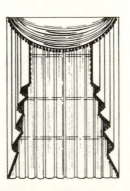

Fringe Swag with Floor Length Cascades

Café Tiered Curtains

BLACKOUT draperies are made from a special material that will eliminate most of the light and heat that can come in through a window. They are hung next to the window on separate traverse rods so that they can be adjusted to give the most flexible control of the environment. Generally, they are used in a double-hung treatment with an overdrapery of a decorative fabric.

CURTAINS are panels of lightweight or sheer material that are sewn together and hung *next to the glass*. They may be used alone, with valances, or with valances and side draperies of heavier material. They are usually stationary and are used in treatment over double-hung windows, picture windows, and glass walls that do not open. However, if preference dictates, they may be hung on rods that allow the option to open.

Typical curtain styles include shirred glass, ruffled tiebacks, and cafés. SHIRRED GLASS curtains are made of a translucent material and are gathered across the top. RUFFLED TIEBACKS are single or crisscross curtains of a sheer fabric that are shirred across the top, edged with a ruffle, and held to each side with tiebacks. CAFÉS are short curtains hung in double or multiple tiers. The tops are pleated or scalloped if decorative rods and rings are used; otherwise the curtain is shirred onto the rod.

VALANCES are short horizontal draperies or facings of fabric, wood, or metal that are stretched across the top of a window treatment as a decorative addition.

FABRIC valances are made from goods that is the same or contrasting with the draperies. They are often trimmed with braid, fringe, or tassels and, depending on the style, may have headings that are plain, pleated, or shirred. They are hung from rods in the same manner as draperies or curtains. Fabric valances that hang in loops or curves are called SWAGS, JABOTS, or FESTOONS, and SHAPED valances are separate fabric panels cut in specified designs.

WOOD (CORNICES) and METAL valances are finished to correspond with the style of the window treatment. They may be painted colors to match or contrast with the room, given natural finishes, or covered with paper or fabric. Brackets support them and fasten them above the draperies or curtains.

TIEBACKS are sashes, tapes, ribbons, or chains used to hold curtains or draperies to the side by scooping the panels into place. The sash type is usually made from the drapery or curtain material, although it may contrast to match a color in the pattern or trim.

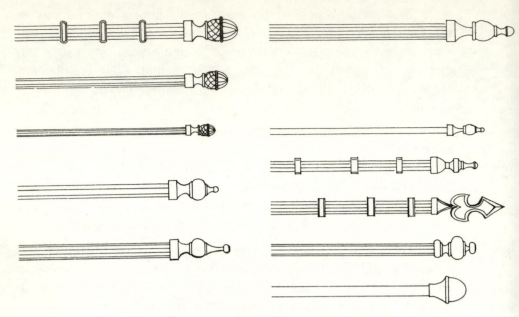

**Types of Decorative Poles and
Finials**

RINGS

White Plastic

Brass Café Clip-on

Metal Fluted Pole

HOOKS

Track Section

Standard Pin

French

French

Pin

HARDWARE

The style of the window treatment dictates the hardware, yet the hardware is the foundation of the treatment.

RODS are especially versatile as they can be adapted to any size or shape of window including bays, bows, and arches. They are adjustable in length and can be expanded even further through the insertion of an extension section. If necessary, they can be custom cut to specified measurements.

A CONVENTIONAL TRAVERSE is a hollow rod encasing a cord and pulley system. The rod is fitted with CARRIERS into which the drapery hooks are fastened and there should be a carrier for each hook, excluding the return. The carriers may be added or removed as needed, and they are supplied with the rod when it is purchased. Master carriers, attached to the cords, force the movement of the drapery along the rod and create an overlap at the meeting point so that the panels will hang together. Rods are manufactured with the pull specified to either side or to the center, and they are usually white in color since the rod is covered when the drapery is closed. The rod is supported by special brackets that may be attached to the ceiling, the wall, or the window casing.

A MOTORIZED ROD is a conventional traverse that uses an electromagnetic motor to move the draperies instead of a cord and pulley system. It can move wide or heavy draperies easily and can be operated with a remote control unit if the draperies are on windows that are high or hard to reach.

The DECORATIVE TRAVERSE has a mechanism like the conventional rod, but instead of carriers, it has sliding RINGS to hold the hooks. The rings are supplied with the rod; again there should be one ring per hook, excluding the return. The drapery hangs below the rod with the headings level with the base of the rings so that the rod is exposed at all times. The rod and rings are given attractive finishes, and the ends of the rods are trimmed with finials of various sizes and shapes. The rod is hung from brackets, and it is recommended that it be mounted on the wall *only*.

A CAFÉ ROD is a metal or wooden pole with a decorative finish and finials trimming the ends. The curtains are hung on rings that slip over the rod and that are manually adjusted. They may be fastened to the rings by sewing or with clips, or they may be attached by slipping hooks through eyes on special rings. The rings, which are purchased separately, should be one-fourth to one-half inch larger in diameter than the rod, and they are usually of the same finish. This type of rod is most often used in pairs to hang short draperies or cafe curtains with one rod at the top and the other at the center of the window. Brackets mounted on the wall or the window casing cradle the rod. Long or short stationary side draperies are also hung from a café rod. For this treatment, the rod is secured above the window and extended beyond its edges.

A CURTAIN ROD is a plain, smooth bar that holds stationary treatments. These treatments usually consist of top-hemmed curtains that are slipped over the rod and pushed together to create fullness. The rod is mounted by brackets either inside or outside the casing.

A SPRING TENSION ROD is a hollow, sectioned curtain rod with a spring inside. The spring allows the rod to depress so that it can be adjusted to fit tightly inside a window casing. The ends are rubber tipped to prevent slipping and marring of the window frame.

BRACKETS are projecting supports for drapery rods, usually three inches long. They are styled to match the various rods and they can hold from one to three rods that may or may not be alike. If the rod length is considerable, extra supports may be added at measured intervals along the rod as well as behind where the draperies stack back.

HOOKS fasten the drapery to the carriers or rings and are attached to the drapery by being sewn or pinned in or by being slipped into the heading hems. A hook with the curve near the top is used if the drapery is to be hung below decorative or ceiling rods. Otherwise the curve should be in the bottom half of the hook so that the heading will cover the rod. For a pleated heading, there should be a hook at each pleat and at each side hem. Scalloped headings have a hook at each point and at both side hems.

HOLDBACKS are ornamental hardware pieces with concealed arms that keep the draperies in place.

TIEBACK HOLDERS are decorative pieces of hardware with nail-like protuberances. They are fastened through the tieback and then embedded into the wall, thus holding the tieback in place.

CUPHOOKS serve the same function as a tieback holder except that the tieback is hung over the hook and it is not visible.

WEIGHTS are small, heavy objects inserted in the drapery or curtain hem to give it stability. DRAPERY weights are thin, flat, smooth pieces of metal encased in cloth. CURTAIN weights are shot pieces sewn into a continuous cloth strip.

CONSTRUCTION

Drapery construction is an exact operation that requires attention to detail. It demands accurate measurements, a wise fabric selection, precise cutting, and proper seaming.

The dimensions of the drapery for a specified window depend upon the treatment and the rod type as well as the size of the window. Each window should be measured separately, as lengths and widths vary as much as one to two inches.

The LENGTH of a drapery is established by the window treatment as draperies may be floor length, window length, or multiple tiered. Allowances must be added to this measurement for heading and hems. The preferred depth for a heading is four or five inches. A finished hem should be a double thickness from three to five inches deep; therefore, from six to ten inches is needed.

The WIDTH of a drapery is the amount of fullness needed to cover the window. It is based on the width of the window plus the distance the treatment extends beyond the window (if it does). The measurement is doubled or tripled depending upon the width and weight of the fabric. To this figure is added the allowances for side hems, overlaps, and returns. A SIDE HEM is usually a double one-inch hem which will require four inches for both side hems for each section. OVERLAPS are the parts of the draperies that extend over each other in the center when the draperies are drawn. Three inches must be added to each section of a two-way draw to accommodate overlapping. A RETURN is the measurement from the rod to the wall based on the length of the bracket. Usually, three inches are added to each drapery section to provide for the return.

The amount of fabric required for the treatment is calculated from the measurements. If the fabric is printed, extra material must be purchased to allow matching of the pattern. The pattern must be continuous across seamed panels, and each pair of panels must be exactly alike. If there is more than one set of panels in a room, all panels must be identical, with the pattern position the same on each.

Fabric for draperies and curtains is available in a wide variety of weaves, colors, and designs. Almost any fabric is appropriate for draperies, but the choice is necessarily limited by several factors: the area where the drapery is to be used, the size and shape of the windows, the direction of the exposure, and the climate of the region.

Weave is also an important consideration. If the fabric is too heavy, it will be difficult to sew, and it may cause hanging problems. Weaves that are too open tend to pull apart at the seams, to have swaying hems, and to stretch or shrink depending upon the weather conditions.

LININGS are the materials used to cover the inner surfaces of the draperies. They are added to give stability to loose weaves, to provide extra weight so that the fabric will retain the shape of the folds, and to protect the fabric from fading and the heat of the sun. Fabric for the lining should be purchased at the same time as the drapery fabric. The yardage is based on the size of the drapery sections and must be figured from those measurements. To find the length of a lining panel three inches is subtracted from the length of the drapery panel for single-hemmed draperies and six is subtracted for double-hemmed. The width of the lining is five inches narrower than the width of the drapery section. Linings are made in tandem with the draperies. After the sections are seamed, they are sewn to the drapery along the side seams. Once the lining is attached, the sections are treated as a single unit while the construction is being completed.

INTERLINING is an inner layer of fabric placed between the drapery fabric and the lining. It may be needed as insulation against heat or cold, to retain heat or cool air, or as a method of keeping out light. The interlining is cut exactly to the measurements of the lining except in the length, where it is slightly shorter. To decrease bulkiness, the seams of the interlining are trimmed away before it is sewn to the lining. After the lining and interlining are sewn together, they are handled as one piece.

The fabric should be spread out, right side up, and examined yard-by-yard for flaws BEFORE the piece is cut. A small imperfection may be hidden in a seam or a hem; but if the goods is badly flawed, the entire piece should be returned and a new shipment requested since it is seldom possible to order a second cutting from the same dye lot. *It is important that any flaws be detected prior to cutting* as the mill may refuse to make an exchange and to reorder will require additional cost.

Prior to cutting each panel, the fabric should be TABLED; that is, it should be laid *squarely* on the cutting surface. This is to make certain that all cuts will be on the *straight* of the goods, not the bias. The folds in the finished drapery will not hang properly if they are bias cut. The *right side* of the fabric should be facing *up* with the print, if any, visible during the tabling and cutting operations. This permits the pattern to be matched so that all the panels will be alike.

The machine needle and the thread must be compatible with the fabric; otherwise the seams may pucker or the stitches skip. Selvages must be trimmed off or clipped so that the seams do not pull. Seams between the panels should be OVERCAST or OVERLOCKED (sewn over the edge) to prevent raveling. Bottom hems should be weighted at the two side hems and all panel seams to hold the seams taut, as they tend to draw up, making the folds crooked and the hems uneven.

HEADINGS arrange the fullness of the fabric at the top of the drapery into structured units such as pleats and scallops or into soft folds for shirring. They set the style of the treatment and give it a finished look.

PLEATS are sections of fabric placed in flat double folds of uniform width and pressed or stitched in place. Several types of pleats are used for headings: pinch, French, box, single, tubular, accordion, and special fold.

For a PINCH PLEAT, each fold fullness is divided into three equal sections. The sections are folded into place, stitched across the lower edge, and pressed to preserve the shape.

FRENCH PLEATS are formed in the same manner as pinch pleats, but the pleats are not pressed into definite folds.

BOX PLEAT folds are divided into two equal sections. The section edges are laid together, flat against the drapery, and stitched across the bottom.

SINGLE PLEATS are folded in, at spaced intervals, and pressed to retain the shape.

TUBULAR PLEATS are formed from scallops. A row of large and small scallops, in alternating sizes and with a three-quarter-inch separation between them, is sewn into the top of the drapery. The ends of the small scallops are drawn together and fastened with a clip to form the pleat.

ACCORDION PLEATS are made with a special preformed buckram that is self-pleating. It is inserted in the top hem of the drapery and the pleats are manipulated into place by hand.

SPECIAL-FOLD PLEATS are oversized pleats that allow a large drapery to stack back into a small area.

SCALLOPS are a series of curves or circular segments that can be sewn into a heading to form an ornamental edge.

SHIRRING is the gathering or pushing together of the fabric fullness. The gathers may be permanently arranged by inserting cording of a specified length into the top hem, drawing the material up along the cording, and then fastening the ends of the cording to the fabric. From one to several rows of this shirring may be used depending on the style, the weight of the fabric, and the amount of fullness. Another method for shirring is to push the curtain rod into the top hem and push the fabric along the rod. After the rod is fastened into the brackets, the folds can be evenly distributed along the rod.

**Cartridge Pleated Heading with
Cord Tieback Over Drapery**

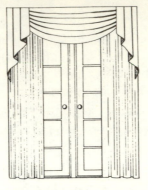

**Plain Swag Heading with
Cascades and Under Drapery**

**Swags with Jabot, Sill Length
Cascades and Tassle Trimming**

**French Pleated Over Drapery
with Borders and French
Pleated Under Curtain**

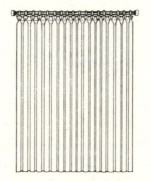

**Butterfly Pleated Heading with
Pole**

**Double Swag with Cascades
and Ruffled Front Drapery**

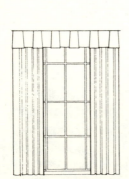

**Box Pleated Valance and
Drapery**

**Sunburst with Rosette, Ruching
and Drapery**

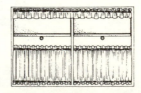

**Dutch Curtains with Shirred
Valance**

INSTALLATION

Draperies are "dressed down" after they are hung; that is, the heading is adjusted and the folds pushed into place. Cotton tape should be tied around pleated drapery and curtain sections at twelve-inch intervals down the length and left for several days. This is to stabilize the pleats so that they will hang in even folds when they are released.

As draperies and curtains hang, they will become acclimated to the temperature, humidity, heating, and air conditioning of the room. This may cause a fluctuation in the hemline. If necessary, the hemline can be adjusted at the job site, either by resewing the hem or by steaming and stretching the fabric.

WORKROOMS

A workroom should be engaged to ensure that the draperies will be manufactured precisely. It is accountable for the entire process, rendering all of the services required to complete a job. Its responsibilities include measuring, inspecting, tabling and cutting, seaming, and installing the window treatment.

Before engaging a workroom, it is good practice to research shops specializing in custom drapery manufacture. The premises should be inspected to determine if the methods are current and if the facilities are clean. The quality of the product should be verified by observing the crew at work and by examining the craftsmanship of a finished drapery. Also, the workroom should adhere to the total-job concept, and it should supply several references if requested.

In addition, the workroom must be willing to work with the designer, discussing the treatment with him so that feasible ideas for achieving a desired effect can be implemented. It should examine the fabric samples he has selected in order to choose the proper material for the design, as such consultations often forestall problems and prevent errors.

Accordion Shade with Banding

WINDOW COVERINGS: SHADES
Definition of Window Shades
Styles
Fabrics
Colors
Measurements
Hardware

A WINDOW SHADE is a piece of stiffened cloth or heavy paper on a spring roller, with a pull to lower and raise it.

A window shade has great versatility because it performs a number of functions without permanently concealing the window or the view. It may shield a window and provide privacy. It can give flexibility in light control by opening wide, softening the light, protecting against glare, or screening out light entirely. It offers insulation against sound, cold, and heat, and it increases the efficiency of heating and air conditioning units.

STYLES

Shades can be adapted to any house, room, or window. They can express any style or design through the choice of fabric, hemline, and trimming as well as through their use with draperies, valances, and sheer or café curtains. And they can be used architecturally to modify the size or shape of a window.

The manner in which the shade is hung must coincide with the design, but the window construction also needs to be considered. To accommodate all possibilities, shades may roll up, down, or sideways, and they may be installed INSIDE the frame for deep-set windows or for windows bordered by handsome woodwork; OVERLAPPING the frame to make small windows look wider or to cover uninteresting windows; FROM CEILING CORNICES to change the dimensions or structure of the window; and FROM TWO DIRECTIONS on the same window for windows that are odd shapes or that have special view problems. In this case two sets of shades are attached — one at the top that pulls down and the other at the bottom that pulls up.

The shape of the HEMLINE is important as it emphasizes the design and style. A hemline may be straight or shaped into any of the wide variety of curved or notched types available. These may follow the pattern of a fabric, repeat a line from the room, or simply accent the design.

Often the lower portion or border of a shade is finished with a TRIM to provide interesting patterns. Trims are made of cotton, silk, or manmade fibers in decorative weaves from one-half to four inches wide. They are manufactured in many shades and may be a single color or combinations of colors.

Types of trimming used on shades are braid and fringe. BRAID is a woven band of cloth, ribbon, or tape. FRINGE is a border or trimming of cords or threads hanging loose or tied in bunches at the top. It may hang in balls, loops, or tassels or combinations of all three.

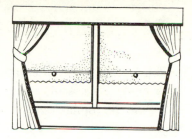

Lambrequin Valance with Over Drapery and Under Shades

Standard Roman Shade

Butterfly Pleated Over Drapery with Shade

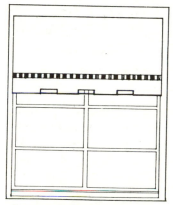

Shade with Banding and Key Cut Out

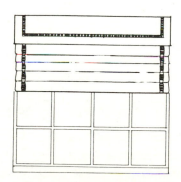

Roman Shade with Valance

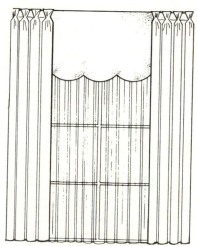

Butterfly Pleated Over Drapery with Scalloped Shade and Under Curtain

FABRICS

Fabrics for window shades must be thin, yet stiff enough to roll easily. Many types are manufactured in a wide variety of textures from smooth to very rough, embroidered, or nubby. They may also be SHEER or translucent to filter the light; DENSE or opaque to darken a room and give maximum protection from light and heat; or DUPLEX which is a double fabric with one design on the inside to coincide with the room and another on the outside to give a uniform appearance to the exterior of the house.

Although shops provide many types of shade fabrics, a specific treatment may require that a particular material be used. To accomplish this, there are several methods available: laminating, stenciling, appliqué-ing, and painting. Through LAMINATING, wallpaper borders and panels or firmly woven fabrics such as cotton or linen are bonded to the window shade material. In STENCILING, ink or paint textile colors are used to apply designs, patterns, or letters to shades. For APPLIQUÉING, motifs from drapery or upholstery fabric are sewn or glued to a shade. PAINT matching a special paint job such as antiqued wood paneling can be applied to a shade to give the desired effect or to complete a design for a wall.

Generally, window shade fabrics are washable, waterproof, and colorfast. It is also important to note that some window shade fabrics are flameproof and will meet government specifications if this is a requirement.

COLORS

Color is chosen to match or contrast with the walls, to repeat the color of the carpet, draperies, or upholstery, to supply a major color contrast, and to correct daylight problems. Shades of color are limitless and may be plain, striped, or blended into designs for scenics, prints, or florals.

MEASUREMENTS

Initially, the length of both sides of the window should be measured to determine if there are any discrepancies in its shape. Then, to find the dimensions for the shade, the window should be remeasured for specifics. If the brackets are to be attached OUTSIDE the frame, the length is measured from the position of the brackets to the sill, and the width equals the width of the frame plus any extension beyond. If the brackets are to be attached INSIDE the frame, the length equals the window opening measurement from the bottom of the frame to the sill, and the width is measured from jamb-to-jamb at the top of the window. All length measurements must have twelve inches added to allow for the take-up on the roller.

HARDWARE

Hardware for shades is simple and includes only rollers, brackets, and pulls.

Window shades are hung on ROLLERS, wooden cylinders with metal pins on the ends. One pin is stationary while the other swivels. The swiveling pin is fastened to a spring that activates the up and down movement of the shade. This mechanism was perfected and patented in 1864. It was so well designed that almost no changes in its construction have been made. Rollers move in either direction so that there are two types: the STANDARD ROLLER that unrolls the shade UNDER from the BACK and the REVERSE ROLLER that unrolls the shade OVER from the FRONT.

Rollers are mounted on BRACKETS that allow the shade to move freely and smoothly. They must be straight, the correct distance apart, and properly aligned. A leeway of one-sixteenth to one-eighth inch must be allowed for action so that the fabric will not rub. There are several types of brackets available.

A STANDARD BRACKET is a bracket that is placed inside the frame.

An INSIDE EXTENSION BRACKET is a special bracket that is attached inside the frame but that extends out to hold the roller outside the frame.

A SASH RUN BRACKET is to be placed at the top of the track in a double-hung window. It has a special bumper that stops the window when it is raised.

OUTSIDE BRACKETS are brackets to be mounted on the frame or the wall.

COMBINATION BRACKETS will hold both the shade and the curtain rod.

A CEILING BRACKET is a bracket to be mounted on the ceiling.

A DOUBLE BRACKET can hold two shades at once.

A BOTTOM-UP BRACKET mounts the shade on the window sill.

A PULL is a small, often decorative, handle fastened into the hem of a shade. Types of pulls include DROPS, TASSELS, RINGS, and CLIP-ONS. They are made from a variety of materials such as metal, plastic, and enamel.

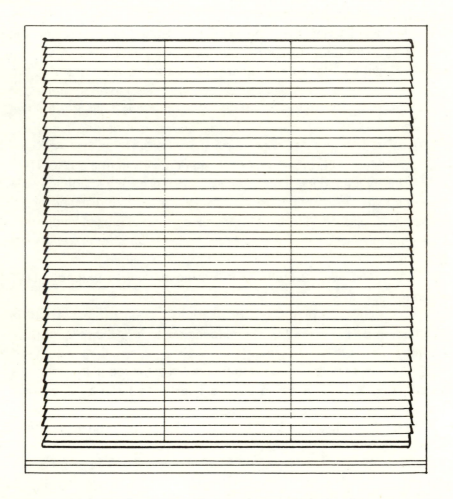

Blind

WINDOW COVERINGS: BLINDS

Definition of Blinds
Styles
Framing
Color
Components
       Slats
       Ladders
       Lift Cord
       Barbs
       Bottom Rail
       Tilter
       Header
       Brackets
Measurement

WINDOW COVERIGNS: BLINDS

BLINDS are window coverings made from a number of thin, horizontal slats that can be set together at any angle or drawn together by means of cords.

Blinds have an important asset in their ability to tilt. They may be set at a slant from slight to great, yet there is always complete visibility. They can be tilted to reflect light in or out, thereby controlling both the glare and the temperature of a room. In addition, they perform the same functions as any other window covering; they provide privacy, control the sun, insulate, and increase the efficiency of heating and air conditioning units.

STYLES

Blinds fit everywhere. They can cover a window, divide a room, enclose a closet, hide an opening, or act as a door. They are a versatile component as they can create an illusion; thus, a room can be "remodeled" without actually changing the structure. They are also desirable for their adaptability to unusual shapes and sizes because the slats can be trimmed to conform to the area where they are to be hung.

FRAMING

FRAMING creates a setting for a blind by changing the shape or the dimensions of the window area. A frame may be added to the window only, or a floor-to-ceiling frame, similar to a screen, may be built around the window and the adjacent wall. Sometimes the framing is accomplished through color. By painting the frame and ledges around the window a color that accentuates the blinds, an effective frame can be achieved.

COLOR

There is an extensive list of baked enamel colors for blinds as well as polished and brushed aluminum. Usually, blinds are solid colors with matching cords and ladders. If it is necessary to have uniformity of color from a viewpoint outside the house, slats may be two-toned.

Much can be done with color to create special effects. Combinations may be used in which slats of differing colors are alternated, blinds reflecting accent colors are interspersed, or tapes of contrasting colors are used. Appliqués of plastic, fabric, or wallpaper may be fastened to the slats with glue. Slats may also be painted on or used in a graphic when the entire window wall is being treated as a unit.

COMPONENTS

Blinds have many parts that, when strung together, work as a unit. These are slats, ladders, lift cords, barbs, bottom rails, tilters, headers, and brackets.

SLATS are usually made from metal and are slightly convex in shape. The standard width is less than an inch, and these narrow slats seem to be preferred as they all but disappear when they are opened, but two-inch slats are also available. There are special slats perforated with tiny pin-holes that can be used to create interesting light effects.

Slats are mounted in braided polyester LADDERS or supports. These may be narrow cords or two-inch-wide tapes.

A LIFT CORD runs through the ladders and slats to fasten them together and to make them maneuverable. For very large, heavy, or difficult to reach blinds, a motorized lift may be used to raise and lower the blinds. A CORD LOCK keeps the blind at the desired level.

BARBS are special hooks at the ends of the ladders that hold them in place so that the slats will remain level and even in length.

The BOTTOM RAIL is a slotted, oval, tubular slat used at the bottom of the blind. The cord lift is knotted into it, and the ladders are secured to it with ladder caps. Its heavier weight helps give stability to the blind.

The TILTER adjusts the slant of the blind and may be positioned on either side. It can be a continuous cord strung through a pulley mechanism that sets the tilt when it is pulled from either of its ends; a wand attached to a gear that regulates the angle of the slats as it is rotated; a sensor, activated by the degree of light, that controls the blind tilt; or a motorized tilting gear.

The HEADER is a boxlike section at the top of the blind that provides a channel to house all the mechanisms that operate it.

There are several types of BRACKETS to be used with blinds: installation, end braces, intermediary, and hold-down.

INSTALLATION BRACKETS are used to fasten the blind inside a frame. There is a cover that snaps on and is secured with a screw. When this screw is tightened, the head of the blind is locked securely in place.

END BRACES are used to install a blind outside the frame. They have adjustable end tabs to keep the blind centered on the window and to hold the header rigid.

INTERMEDIARY BRACKETS are support brackets placed at intervals on wide blinds to prevent sagging.

HOLD-DOWN BRACKETS are placed at each end of the bottom rail to keep the blind from swaying when a door is opened or closed. They may be secured to a hook at the top of the sill, inside the jamb, to the face of the frame, or to a door or wall.

MEASUREMENTS

Measurements for blinds, like other window coverings, are determined from their position at the window. For blinds to be hung INSIDE the frame, the width is measured as the exact distance between the inside edges of the window casing, and the length is the exact distance between the inside edge of the soffit and the place designated for the bottom edge of the blind. For blinds to be hung OUTSIDE the window frame, the width is the exact distance between the point where the brackets are to be placed (Brackets need a one-inch-wide, flat surface for mounting), and the length is the exact distance between the top of the bracket and the location of the bottom of the blind.

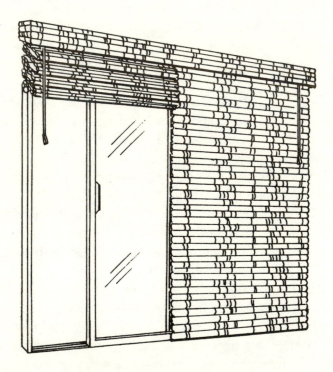

Pair of Shades on One Window

WINDOW COVERINGS: WOVEN SHADES

Definition of Woven Shades
Styles
Construction
Colors
Installation

WINDOW COVERINGS: WOVEN SHADES

A WOVEN SHADE is a window covering made from narrow slats interwoven with yarn.

A woven shade is unusually adaptable and can accommodate many treatments and installations. If offers a solution for coverings of doors, windows, and openings where other materials might be impractical or unworkable. Besides, it provides flexible light control, natural insulation against heat and cold, and seclusion. It may be used effectively to create or enclose space, to produce a tapestry effect, and to effect the visual impact of a room.

STYLES

Woven shades have borrowed everything but their fabric from other types of window coverings. They may be installed as Roman shades, spring roller shades, cord and pulley shades, draperies, valances, cáfe curtains, room dividers and folding doors, and canopies.

In the ROMAN SHADE style, the woven material forms large accordion pleats as it is raised. The shade is fastened over the window by a HEADRAIL, and it is operated by a pull cord that may be on either side. There is an attached VALANCE that covers the hardware only, and the valance and the SKIRT or hemline of the shade may be trimmed. A wider DUSTCAP and a deeper valance must be ordered if the shade is to be hidden when it is raised. VALANCE RETURNS, flaps of material that cover the headrail ends, are suggested if an outside or ceiling mount installation is used.

A DOUBLE-FOLD ROMAN SHADE is a Roman shade that may be *either* lowered by top-lowering cords on the left or raised by bottom-raising cords on the right. It has a six-inch front valance which, along with the skirt, may be trimmed.

For SPRING ROLLER SHADES, the woven fabric is attached to a heavy spring roller and the shade is operated like an ordinary window shade. A valance is not included, but one may be ordered separately. Trimming may be added to both the hemline and the valance.

As a CORD AND PULLEY SHADE, the woven fabric rolls at the bottom as it is raised. This is accomplished by vertical cords that run from the front to the back. Both sides of the shade should be identical as the reverse side is visible as the shade rolls up. A valance is included and it may be plain or trimmed, as desired.

Outside Mount

Inside Mount

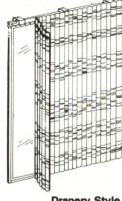
Drapery Style

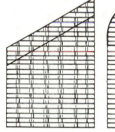
Angle Top

Cathedral   Canopy

Spring Roller Shade

Café Curtain

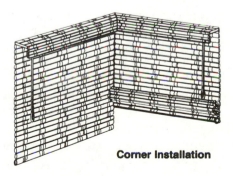
Corner Installation

DRAPERIES may be made from the woven material by turning it sideways so that the yarns run horizontally and the slats are vertical and can stack to the side. Pleats are made with pleater tape, and pin hooks are used for hanging. This type of drapery is heavy so it must be hung on special traverse rods. It may be a one-way panel or have a center-pair opening.

Stand-alone VALANCES to be used over woven or fabric window coverings or by themselves may be made from the flat, vertical material. It is mounted on a dustcap and has attached endcaps. Both the top and bottom edges are finished with gimp.

CAFÉ CURTAINS are made in the same way as draperies, except that the curtains are hung with brass café clips on decorative rods. The top edge is finished with gimp.

ROOM DIVIDERS and FOLDING DOORS are also manufactured like the draperies with vertical slats and horizontal yarns. The fullness is arranged by pleats that are positioned during the manufacturing process. The dividers and folding doors slide on nylon carriers that are attached to the slats and that fit into a flanged track. The vertical ends are finished with rails — one to act as an anchor and stabilizer and the other, fitted with handles, to be a lead rail.

CANOPIES may be used alone or with window coverings. They are mounted to a headrail and are stretched to a pole decorated at the ends with finials. The proper drop and projection are maintained by curved metal supports. A plain or trimmed skirt may be added below the finials.

As with other window coverings, woven shades can easily be adapted to special shapes and sizes. The valance for the shade can be mitered to fit the angles in corners, bay windows, and alcoves. A SINGLE HEADRAIL with a continuous valance may be used as the mounting for several shades. This is an especially versatile treatment as each shade operates separately and one treatment can be used to cover both the doors and the windows in a single wall. CURVED STATIONARY VALANCES can handle arches and cathedral windows that need a window covering that will accommodate the curve. The shade hangs below the valance and can open only to the point where the pleat stack meets the bottom of the valance. The valance is outlined with gimp to finish the edges. ANGLED VALANCES may be shaped to fit slanted ceilings or windows. The valance may be angled across the top only or across both the top and the bottom, and all the angled edges are finished with gimp. The shade hangs below the angle and can be raised only to this point.

CONSTRUCTION

Woven shades are constructed by interweaving slats and yarn to form the covering material. SLATS are long, flat pieces, usually made of wood or aluminum, ranging in width from one-fourth to almost one inch. YARN is made from both natural and man-made fibers that have been spun or twisted into novelty styles.

The SKIRT or bottom edge of both the shade and the valance may be straight or shaped into various styles of scallops. Basic scallops have a cut-out depth of three inches from the edge and are curved, angular, or combinations of both. Elevated scallops are raised above the bottom of the shade and are only outlined, not cut out. The scallops are proportioned to the shade width, and all shades in a room are treated alike. Separate shades hanging together are treated as one.

TRIMS may be added to most of the shade, valance, or canopy types to accentuate the style of a room and to personalize the effect. They may be made from natural or man-made fibers, usually cotton or rayon, and they are color coordinated with the shade or room. Trims used on woven shades include gimp, fringe, or tassels. GIMP is used to finish the edge of a shade or valance by applying a single outline row or several rows equally spaced. FRINGE may be attached to the edge of the woven material so that the fringes hang freely below it. TASSELS may be added as extra decoration along with the gimp. The tassels may be either a separate unit fastened to the material or a self-tied unit in which the yarns from the shade are extended and hand tied into a six-inch tassel.

COLORS

Colors supplied by the manufacturer are chosen to coordinate with fabrics, furniture, and accessories. Yarns are pressure dyed to color, and wooden slats are stained to retain the grain and natural wood characteristics or painted shades to match the other colors being used in the room. Aluminum slats may be a natural metal finish or glazed with color. These components are interwoven into many designs that will complement the colors of most interiors.

INSTALLATION

Installation of woven wood window coverings parallels those of other types of coverings to which they are similar. Measurements and hardware specifications have already been discussed in those sections and should be referred to when necessary.

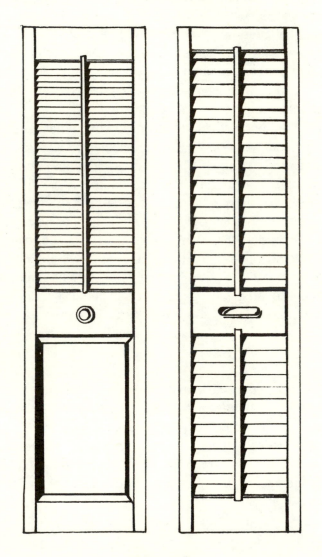

Shutter Doors

WINDOW COVERINGS: SHUTTERS

Definition of Shutters

Styles

Construction

      Stiles

      Rails

      Inserts

Hardware

Colors

Installation

Measurements

WINDOW COVERINGS: SHUTTERS

A SHUTTER is a movable screen or cover for a window, usually hinged and fitted with movable louver or solid inserts.

Shutters are window coverings with permanence. As they are generally made from wood that has been finished, they will resist the effects of the elements — sun, heat, humidity, smoke, dampness — that deteriorate other types of materials. Additionally, they are strong and will withstand movement and position changes. They adjust to let in the light, to permit a view of the scenery, and to catch the breezes, yet they offer privacy.

STYLES

Although shutters are a decorative window covering, they are often designed to coincide with the building and room architecture. Specifications may designate the number of divider rails, the types of inserts, the choice of beading, and the details of the header.

Shutters may be window size and fill only the window opening, or they may expand to the width of a wall and be full length, extending to the floor. Thus, they are a useful and practical method for covering windows, screening doorways, dividing rooms, and enclosing areas.

CONSTRUCTION

Shutters are manufactured from wooden components that are fastened together with dowels and glue or rabbeted joints. These components include stiles, rails, and the several types of inserts.

STILES are the vertical side pieces into which the inserts are fastened. The size of the window and the style of the shutter dictate the width, which may vary from one and three-eighths to two inches. Some designs use beading, a decorative convex curve, along the inside edges of the stiles.

RAILS are horizontal pieces attached to the stiles to form panel frames. The rail across the TOP of the frame is the HEAD. It may be straight across both edges with the bottom edge plain or beaded, or it may have a plain top edge with the lower edge cut into a decorative shape. A DIVIDER RAIL separates the insert sections of the panel. It may be used for a decorative purpose or to give stability to very high panels.

INSERTS are the sections in the center of the frame that complete the panel. A panel may have one or more inserts depending on the designs and styles selected and the size. These may be alike or of differing materials and may include louvers, fabric, mesh, and plastic or wood partitions.

LOUVERS are movable flat or curvilinear blades with width sizes from one and one-quarter to four and one-half inches. The blades may be mounted either vertically or horizontally, and they are adjusted by a wand attached at the edge in the center of the louver. Although each blade is mounted separately, they all work together as a single unit and can be slanted in any direction by merely moving the wand up or down.

FABRIC coordinated with or matching the materials used in a room may be shirred onto a spring tension rod and inserted into the frame.

MESH, consisting of wood, wire, cane, or plastic grilles of parallel, diagonal, or latticed bars, in widths varying from narrow to wide may be cut to the desired dimensions and fastened into the frame to create an openwork panel.

Plain or patterned sections of translucent or opaque PLASTIC, color coordinated or matched to the other materials in the room, may be trimmed to the necessary dimensions and used as inserts.

Spindle and solid WOOD inserts finished to match the frame may complete a panel.

HARDWARE

Hardware for shutters consists of hinges, small pull knobs, and hook latch fasteners. Decorative hardware may be added to the divider rails and inserts as an option at additional cost.

COLORS

Shutters may be finished in one of the standard colors provided by the manufacturer or a custom color matched to a swatch submitted by the designer. They are often made to coincide or blend with the architectural or furniture woods used in a room. This may be achieved with paint or with a stain which will enhance the grain, texture, and color of the wood. Paint may also be used to provide color in contrasting or accenting values.

INSTALLATION

The size and style of the shutter determines the hanging method. Usually, the panels are hinged together and hung as a single unit. Two

 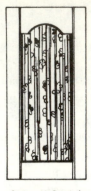 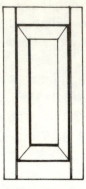 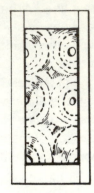

Vertical Louvers   **Shirred Curtain**   **Wood Panel**   **Acrylic Panel**

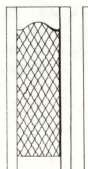

Metal Inserts

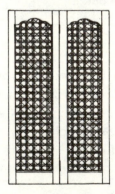 

Cane Inserts   **Wood Weave Inserts**

Shutter Styles

units of equal size may be double-hung over the window, while very large and full-length units are fastened to tracks or casters. It is necessary that there be a clearance between the glass and the shutter to allow for protruding louvers. Therefore, shutters are usually fastened to hanging strips which are mounted directly on the wall or over the existing molding at the window or doorway.

MEASUREMENTS

The window should be measured at several points along both the length and width, and then the largest dimensions recorded. Double-hung windows should have the top and bottom windows measured separately.

Mounting may be either inside or outside the window casing. Hanging requirements must be considered when the measurements are taken. Shutters attached *inside* should be flush with the window casing after they are hung. A flat surface of one and one-half inches is required for mounting, and one inch is needed for the strips used beside the panels. Generally, the casing is entirely covered in an *outside* installation. This may require special hanging strips that may be custom ordered.

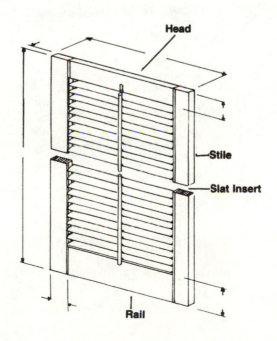

Shutter Construction Detail

PART III

CHAPTER 7 — **WOOD FURNITURE**

CHAPTER 8 — **UPHOLSTERED FURNITURE**

CHAPTER 9 — **ACRYLIC FURNITURE**

CHAPTER 7   WOOD FURNITURE

History of Wood Furniture
Definition
Construction
    Base or Plinth
    Legs, Posts, Rails, Stretchers
      Materials for Legs
      Leg Shapes
    Cases
      Materials for Cases
        Plywood
        Solid Glued-up Stock
        Frame and Panel
        Sticking
      Open Frame
      Dust Panels
    Doors
      Solid
      Light-weight
      Flexible or Tambour
      Folding or Accordion
      Methods for Hanging
    Drawers
      Drawer Sections
      Dividers
      Guides and Runners
    Trays
    Shelves
    Tops
    Cornices
    Chairs
Hardware
The Custom Shop

Wood was a valuable commodity in the ancient world, as some areas were richly endowed and others were almost barren. It was an important item of trade — a record of the Third Egyptian Dynasty (c. 2686–2613 B.C.) shows that forty ships laden with timber landed at Egyptian ports — and cargoes included cedar, cypress, ash, box, and ebony. Wood was also considered an acceptable tribute payment, especially ebony, which was probably the most highly prized.

Ancient Egypt seems to have been the first culture to have produced fine furniture. Some pieces have survived, due largely to burial customs which included them in royal tombs. Craftsmen used the native sidder, acacia, and carob as well as the imported woods to make chests, chairs, benches, and beds. Joints were commonly mortise-and-tenon with wooden dowels or leather thongs to secure them. The arts of veneering, marquetry, and inlay were highly developed and imaginatively used.

Even fewer pieces of Roman and Greek furniture remain. Fortunately, vase paintings and relief sculpture can provide information about style and design. Timber was plentiful for both Roman and Greek artisans and included citron, maple, yew, holly, oak, willow, lime, zygia, and beech. Mortise-and-tenon joints secured with wooden dowels or glue were used. Chair and table legs were often lathe turned, and veneer and inlay decorated the finer pieces.

Naturally, the Egyptian influence is present in the early forms of furniture, but the Greeks gradually developed their own style using rectangular and turned supports. An elegant chair with curving legs and backboard, called Klismos, evolved. The Romans elaborated on the Klismos chair and produced one of similar design but heavier form. They constructed new types of seats, such as paneled benches and wickerwork chairs, and they introduced the chest of drawers. These classic, ancient designs have inspired and influenced artisans through the ages, and rudiments of their work are present even today.

Woodworking was a craft developed early in Chinese history, and by the time of the Han Dynasty (206 B.C.–A.D. 221), the making of furniture was firmly established. The Chinese used varieties of rosewood, satinwood, cedar, elm, and camphor wood. They were masters of joinery and used an elaborate mortise-and-tenon combined with a miter or sometimes a dovetail. They *never* used nails or glue, and dowels only rarely. To solve the expansion and contraction problems, they used "floating" panels.

The types of furniture desired in China differed greatly from those used in the West. Tables served a great variety of functions and were of many sizes and shapes. Some chairs were similar to Western design with a boxlike frame or a curved back while others were made from bent bamboo or had woven cane seats with an underwebbing of palm fiber. They were ornamented with inlay, paint, lacquer, or fretwork. The Chinese were partial to chests and cabinets, preferring to store everything out of sight, and produced numerous types of chests and cupboards.

An interesting contrast to the Chinese are the Japanese, who never felt the need to develop furniture. They preferred to sit on the floor and used low tables with folding legs and small boxes that could be stored in cupboards when not in use.

Primitive societies learned to incorporate the natural characteristics of trees into items of furniture. Seats were formed by arranging logs in place and sticking branches into the ground to form vertical backrests. Branches were laid on the ground to make simple beds. Forked branches were carved into stools or used as the uprights for sleeping platforms, with the forks forming rests into which the cross pieces were fastened. Sometimes large, solid pieces were worked with an adze to form three- or four-legged stools which were used as seats or food receptacles.

One of the most ingenious uses of solid wood was invented by the Indians of the northwest coast of America. They used wedges to split logs into planks. The planks were scored to form the base and sides of a box and were then bent into shape and fastened into position.

The emphasis in furniture making shifted from the East to the West during the Middle Ages. The European countries became the most influential producers although furniture was limited in quantity. Very little early medieval furniture has survived, but paintings contemporary with the time have preserved its descriptions. It was clumsy and crude, having been hewn from oaken timbers and decorated with tracery, arcades, and columns such as those used by stonemasons. However, toward the end of the Middle Ages, southern Europe, especially Italy and Germany, developed expertise in painted decoration.

This was the ''Age of the Joiner,'' and the craft of furniture making gradually developed more sophistication. New types of joints were invented and employed, which culminated in the making of better and more beautiful pieces. Plank construction was used for the earliest furniture, but this eventually evolved into the more elaborate panel-and-frame.

Since practicality was the most important consideration in medieval furniture, emphasis was focused on the making of chests. The dug-out, hewn by an ax or adze from a solid bulk of timber, was one of the earliest types. Plank construction followed this. It allowed more interior

space and was lighter and easier to move. The end panels had vertical grain while the grain ran horizontally on the rest of the pieces. Chests rested on the floor, but gradually the side panels began to be extended to raise the body and provide legs. Leather straps formed hinges and dowels held the panels in place.

Clamp-fronted chests were made from panels tenoned into each other and secured with wooden pegs. The side panels were also tenoned and then braced by stout crosspieces. Lids were attached with dowels which allowed them to pivot. The ark chest was, in essence, a clamp-front chest with a raised lid made from three planks held in place by shaped endpieces.

The rounded-lid chest was also popular at this time. It had sides of stout planks that were spiked together and banded with iron strips. The inside of a half log was hollowed out to form the rounded lid.

The paneled chest employed the most refined techniques. Insert panels were set into frames without gluing or pinning. This helped solve the splitting problem which had long troubled craftsmen. The sections were joined with tenons or wooden dowels or both. Most of these chests were decorated either with carved ornamentation or painting.

The most important article of furniture was the bed. Its size and ornateness was a sign of the monetary value of its owner. A large framework surrounded the bed, and it was enclosed with textile hangings. After the advent of frame and panel construction, the box bed was utilized. This was an enclosed bed made entirely of wood, often elaborately carved or inlaid, with cupboards above and below for storage. It combined utility and comfort as the bed was warm in those days which antedated the central heating system.

Besides the chest and the bed, trestle tables that could be readily dismantled and stacked away were used. Stools, benches, and folding chairs that were easily movable were important articles in the household as well. This knock-apart and portable design was the result of two important influences in medieval life. First, the great hall in which the furniture was housed was the center of activity and had to accommodate many purposes. Second, living conditions in those times were very unsettled and it was often necessary to pack hurriedly and find other lodgings.

The design of some chairs was derived from the chest and also used the plank technique. An interesting innovation was the box chair, a chest with arms and a back. It was of panel construction and had a hinged seat or panel which allowed access to the storage space underneath.

In the early days, the chair was a sign of high social rank, and only those persons possessing such distinction used them. During the sixteenth century, backrests began to be added to the stools of more common folk. The name "backstool" was given to these new pieces of furniture so as not to offend the nobility.

The backstool was the harbinger of the Windsor chair, the first chair to be used by everyone. It had turned legs and back supports that were set into holes bored into the seat. It was made of many different woods, with seats of elm or oak, legs of beech, birch or fruitwood, and back hoops of yew that were bent into shape by steaming. A type of mass production was devised to produce the chair. Each part was made by craftsmen who specialized in a particular section. The finished sections were sent to cottage workshops where the parts were assembled.

A new creative vigor arose in Italy during the fourteenth century. Furniture began to resemble the house for which it was intended and cabinetmaking, especially, became a fine art. The wood from which the furniture was made also became a decorative feature and the art of inlay was developed. Carving was an important ornamental form and large, sweeping flora, fauna, foliage, animal masks, female busts, and shells were used.

Italian furniture was much admired by other countries, and the craftsmen were invited to foreign cities to exchange ideas, styles, and skills. Old methods were improved and new ones were developed as designs to satisfy a great variety of tastes evolved. Fine furniture production, particularly cabinetmaking, began to flourish over most of Europe.

Dutch and Flemish artisans became masters at working with ebony. The rarity of this wood required that it be used as veneer and cabinetmakers traveled to Flanders to learn the art of veneering with this very hard, fine wood. Certain elements of style were borrowed from the Dutch as well. They used beveled panels in frames and applied moldings and turned posts cut in half lengthwise to flat surfaces to create geometric designs. This influence is found in both English and American cabinetry.

France was to assume the leadership in furniture development through the next periods. King Louis XIV appointed Charles LeBrun as Chief of Arts and Crafts. LeBrun established a furniture factory at Gobelins which became the foremost company of cabinetmakers of the time. Each piece of furniture was a work of art, as only master craftsmen were employed there.

The work at the factory was to continue through the reigns of several monarchs. One of the most notable cabinetmakers worked during the reign of Louis XV, André Charles Boulle. He developed veneering to perfection, especially with tortoise shell and brass. Most of the other furniture pieces were heavily carved, silvered or gilded, and veneered.

Early in the eighteenth century, changes began to take place.

Furniture became lighter, more subtle, elegant, and feminine. Decoration was carried to great extremes and bronzework, originally intended to protect the furniture, was added everywhere. This style eventually waned and furniture became more subdued, yet it retained its graceful and elegant style.

The next trend favored purer classical design based on Grecian and Roman influences and the decoration was now subordinate to the design. Walnut, mahogany, satinwood, ebony, and many exotic woods for inlay work were the lumbers used. Parquetry in both geometric and floral designs became a prominent method of ornamentation, and veneering over curved surfaces was perfected. The furniture produced during this period is linked with Louis XVI, and it reached a high level of excellence.

After the Revolution, everything previously held in high esteem was discarded, even quality and workmanship. Consequently, the art of furniture making in France declined.

Paralleling the trends on the Continent were the advances in cabinetmaking that developed in England. When Henry VIII came to the throne, a new awareness was beginning to pervade the country. Henry promoted the arts and had a huge palace built to compete with those of the Continent. He furnished it lavishly, commissioning cabinetmakers to produce special pieces. His daughter, Queen Elizabeth I, furthered this interest and, under her leadership, furniture assumed the English style.

Both monarchs encouraged Italian, Flemish, and French craftsmen to settle in England where they could teach their skills to local cabinetmakers. They ratified trade agreements allowing furniture to be imported. Designs from these pieces were copied and modified to produce England's own interpretation of the new styles.

Furniture development during the reigns of James I and Charles I retained the old forms but subdued the lavish carving and used plainer designs. The Restoration marked a new age for furniture as it became more luxurious and complicated. Walnut was the most favored wood, although oak, elm, yew, and beech were also used. Chairs were highly decorated with turning and carving, and the oval gate-leg table appeared.

Highly decorative Chinese and Japanese furniture became popular. A mongrel style, which bore the Oriental influence but which was not authentic design, developed. It permeated every type of furniture — chairs, chests, tables, and beds. Even the decoration was in the Chinese manner with lacquer and gilding.

There was a gradual return to a simpler style with the accession of Queen Anne. Matched walnut veneers were used on cabinets until the walnut famine in France forced the use of mahogany. Mahogany was not favored for veneering, but it carved well, and it became an important wood for furniture making. The cabriole leg was established as the normal chair leg and several styles of feet were developed.

About this time, individual artisans broke from anonymity to achieve fame as outstanding cabinetmakers. This is partly because they published books about furniture. The best known was Thomas Chippendale, who is remembered especially for the high quality of his workmanship. His first efforts were renditions of his own designs; however, within a decade he was working in the designs of Robert Adam. Adam had a profound impact on the design of furniture, and he insisted that the designs be rendered with crisp, lively carvings and master craftsmanship. Other cabinetmakers in this publishing spree were William Hallett, William Ince, George Hepplewhite, and Thomas Sheraton.

Styles again began to turn, and the cabriole leg was replaced by tapered, square-cut legs. Marquetry and painted panels were used for decoration, and the Carleton House writing table was devised.

Trees abounded in colonial America, and early settlers used the native wood, especially pine, oak, and maple, to construct furniture to fulfill their utilitarian needs. Parts often had to be whittled as the simple machines used to turn legs or spokes were very scarce. Wooden pegs were used to assemble the parts as there were few metal nails. Again, the chest was the most important piece of furniture, serving as a seat, table, and desk as well as a storage unit.

Arriving settlers brought furniture with them, and the colonial pieces became more varied and ornate. The chest evolved into a chest-on-chest. A larger top was added to chests of drawers to create writing desks. Designs progressed from heavy, sturdy pieces to lighter, more practical types. The wood lathe was imported and beautiful turned posts and legs were developed. Craftsmen created the hutch cabinet, the cobbler's bench, the butterfly table, and the long trestle table.

American furniture in the early eighteenth century derived its style largely from prominent English cabinetmakers such as Chippendale, Sheraton, Hepplewhite, and Adam. Only one American artisan, Duncan Phyfe, developed a characteristic style. He created pieces with fine carving and reeding, a pedestal table with three or four legs, a lyre-back chair, and a bronze claw to be used at the ends of legs.

The first half of the nineteenth century saw the revival or reinterpretation of previous periods both in Europe and America. There was some variation in ornamentation, especially in Victorian furniture which, at first, was generally plain and then became more intricate. Veneer cutting techniques continued to improve, and French masters focused on achieving decorative effects with natural grains, colors, and figures.

As technology advanced, new and improved processes influenced the furniture industry. When machines began to imitate the fine hand work of the craftsman, the quality of the pieces deteriorated. Mechanization stripped the personalized characteristics from the pieces. Early modern designers tried to establish a new trend which only succeeded in producing sharp angles and harsh lines.

Today, a more fluid, subtle style with distinctive qualities using many materials such as wood, metal, glass, plastic, ceramics, and cane, has emerged. Contemporary furniture is distinguished by its flexibility, its compactness, and its usefulness. It is simple and functional with little carving or other design, and most of it is given a natural finish.

DEFINITION

Furniture made from wood is a unique combination of science and art. Science is required to engineer its structure so that it will have stability and durability and so that the most expedient use of its special properties will be made. Art gives furniture style and beauty, elements that are achieved through design, decoration, color, and finish. It enhances the natural characteristics of wood through the creative use of materials and techniques. From the union of these components come appealing and satisfying pieces of furniture.

CONSTRUCTION

Wood furniture is constructed from components that are built as separate sections and then joined together. Usually, there is a base or a leg assembly to support the piece. A BASE or PLINTH is an enclosed, hollow, rectangular frame that may be a simple, straight design or a molded shape. It should be approximately two to four inches high, and it is often recessed.

LEGS, POSTS, RAILS, STRETCHERS

LEGS, POSTS, RAILS, and STRETCHERS are essential structural parts on many kinds of furniture. They may be a major design feature, and they often identify a definite style. They are made in various lengths and shapes and are generally cut from solid wood, although laminated materials are also used. Solid wood is preferable as it yields a sturdy one-piece section that has no glue line to break or glue joint to show. Also, it gives uniformity of color. Leg shapes follow particular forms and are square, round, turned, cabriole, and tripod.

SQUARE LEGS have angular corners. They may be straight, having the same dimensions along the entire length, or tapered on the two inside surfaces to give a feeling of lightness for contemporary furniture. Traditional and provincial furniture have square legs that are tapered on all four sides.

ROUND LEGS, usually found on contemporary furniture, are tapered and are often finished with brass ferrules and self-leveling bases.

TURNED LEGS and posts are made up of combinations of shapes and may vary from simple to very ornate. Surfaces may be square, tapered, coved or concavely curved, beaded or convexly curved, and filleted or grooved with short, straight lines that separate the different parts. Sections may be of equal or different lengths, and there are usually two or more sections per leg or post.

CABRIOLE LEGS are S-shaped and are characteristic of eighteenth-century furniture. They are varied in style with the English version emphasizing the knee and the French version concentrating on a graceful foot and ankle. Cabriole legs to be attached to rectangular surfaces have square tops, and those to be used with circular or oval shapes have cat-faced tops.

TRIPOD LEGS have a central stem or pedestal from which three short legs extend.

Further ornamentation may be added to legs by making special decorative cuts at equal intervals along the length of a surface. The convex spaces are called REEDING, and the concave spaces are called FLUTING.

Leg assemblies are constructed by joining legs to rails or aprons, the rails under a table top that connect the legs together. Sometimes low rails or STRETCHERS are added for extra strength. Traditionally, legs and rails have been joined with blind mortise-and-tenon joints. Other possible constructions are the dovetail-dado, which is a good lock joint, and the butt joint strengthened with two or three dowels and bonded with a good adhesive. To add strength, a wood or metal corner block installed with screws is used.

CASES

To the finished base is added a unit which usually consists of a CASE fitted with doors, drawers, or shelves and special internal details. Oftentimes, the taller pieces of furniture consist of two or more case units piled one atop the other.

The large surfaces for the case, such as the sides, back, tops, and

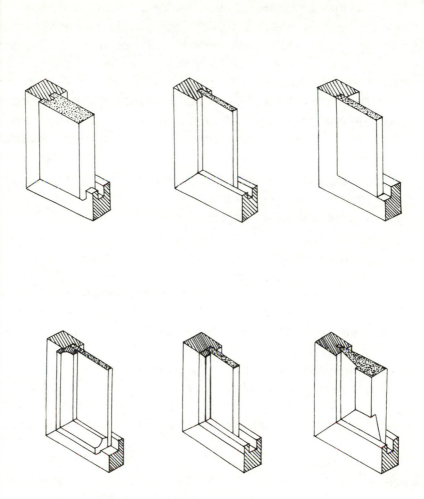

Frame and Panel Construction

shelves, are produced from plywood, solid glued-up stock, or frame-and-panel construction.

Pieces may be cut directly from PLYWOOD as it comes from the mill ready to be used. However, plywood has unattractive edges that do not finish well. If the edges are to be exposed, they should be banded with a material that is prefinished to match the surface or that can be finished to resemble the rest of the piece. BANDS may be strips of thin veneer or plastic laminate that are glued to the flat edge of the wood or thin pieces of solid wood. Flat, solid wood strips may be fastened along the edge with a tongue and groove joint or V-shaped pieces of solid stock may be fitted into matching V-shaped grooves cut into the edge.

SOLID GLUED-UP STOCK refers to material made from strips of solid wood that are glued together and pressed until they are dry. Use of this type of material is limited, as it does *warp*.

FRAME-AND-PANEL CONSTRUCTION consists of a four-sided border structure or FRAME into which a flat piece of material or PANEL is fitted. The frame requires two vertical members called STILES and two horizontal members called RAILS. Sometimes intermediate dividers are used; those running vertically are CROSS or LOCK rails and those running horizontally are CROSS stiles or MULLIONS. The corner joints are mortise-and-tenon or doweled.

The inside edge of the frame is described by the word STICKING and is square or molded. The shape may be cut directly into the frame or it may be devised by adding molding. The edge is also grooved or cut to receive the panel. Groove placement can be varied so that the panel is FLUSH or even with the stiles and rails; STRAIGHT or PLANE which is centered in the edge of the frame; or ELEVATED or RAISED above the frame.

The sides, top, and bottom are usually joined with a lock-miter joint to form a square corner. If the sides overlap at the top and bottom, the pieces may be fitted together with some kind of dado joint or with dowel construction. If the top and bottom overlap the sides, a web or skeleton frame may complete the inner rectangular box; then the pieces are fitted to the frame.

An OPEN or SKELETON FRAME consists of two vertical and two horizontal members that are joined with dowels, mortise-and-tenon joints or a stub-tenon joint. It is installed inside a case to add stability and to provide support. A similar unit divided by rails at specified intervals holds drawers. Horizontal panels or DUST PANELS of plywood or hardboard are often inserted between the rails to keep the drawers dust free.

DOORS

DOORS may enclose the case to provide a beautiful exterior surface and to conceal storage.

SOLID DOORS are made from solid glued-up stock, tongue-and-groove paneling, veneer or lumber-core plywood, hardboard for small sliding doors, glass, and frame-and-panel construction.

If a LIGHTWEIGHT DOOR is needed, honeycomb core construction is used. This consists of a solid wood frame with a filler of paper and plastic and a surface cover of veneer.

FLEXIBLE or TAMBOUR DOORS are made of vertical slats of wood fitted together in such a way that they will slide around corners — either with wooden or plastic joints or mounted on a heavy canvas backing.

FOLDING or ACCORDION DOORS are also made from vertical sections of wood, but they are jointed so that they will fold against one another into a compact unit.

Methods for hanging doors vary in order to conform to the details of design and style.

FLUSH DOORS fit into the face or framework of a case so that the surface is level. To accomplish this, butt, pivot, or decorative surface hinges are used.

The LIP DOOR is hung so that part of the frame or plate is covered, and it requires a semi-concealed hinge.

A door covering two, three, or four edges of the case is called an OVERLAY, and pin or pivot hinges should be used with it.

ROLLING DOORS are mounted into an overhead track and are kept in place by a guide fastened at the bottom.

SLIDING DOORS are set into plastic or metal tracks, both above and below.

Doors that DROP open may be hung with either the flush or lip methods.

Some type of hardware is usually attached to the door front. Again, design and style are factors in its choice and position. However, it is usually placed in a location convenient to reach and use — either near the opening edge or in the center of the door.

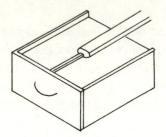

Center Guide

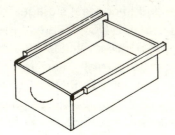

Side Guide

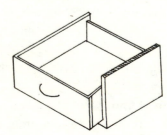

Runner

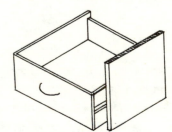

Side Guide

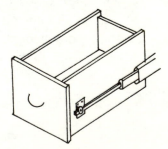

Metal Side Guides

Drawer Guides

DRAWERS

DRAWERS are among the most difficult items to build. They need to be of sound construction to withstand the frequent pulling and pushing. They must be properly designed, because a drawer should slide easily, never stick, pull out far enough for convenient use without tipping or falling, and stay "in square."

Drawer FRONTS are made of solid stock and usually match the case in kind of wood, design, and general appearance. They are often decorated with carving or moldings. The SIDES and BACK of the drawer are made of less expensive wood, either solid stock or plywood. The BOTTOM is made of plywood or hardwood since these materials do not expand or contract with changes in the humidity.

In joining the front to the sides, rabbet, drawer-corner, tongue-lap, mill-shaper, lock, or multiple-dovetail joints are used. The back is attached to the sides with butt, dado, dado-and-lip, dovetail, or rabbet joints. The bottom is usually set into a groove cut into all four sides.

Drawers are often partitioned on the inside by DIVIDERS or section pieces that are cut into all four sides of the drawer.

To keep the drawer in line so that it will move easily and smoothly, a mechanism called a GUIDE is used.

The simplest guide is a RUNNER for the drawer sides. It is a corner-shaped piece set into the frame where the edges of the drawer will run.

SIDE GUIDES and RUNNERS consist of grooves cut into the sides of the drawer which act as slides and are fitted into runners fastened to the sides of the case. This can be reversed with the grooves being cut into the case and the runners being attached to the drawer.

CENTER GUIDES and RUNNERS are made up of pieces of stock with a groove that is attached to the bottom of the drawer and a glide that is fastened into the case frame under the drawer.

Opening devices for drawers may be metal, plastic, or matching wood hardware. Where a non-hardware method is preferred, a RECESS may be cut under or above the front of the drawer, or an OPENING may be cut out at the center of the top edge of the drawer.

TRAYS

TRAYS are small boxes or drawers that fit inside a drawer or cabinet. They are equal in width to the inside of the unit but are shorter from the back to the front. They move on slides fastened inside the drawers or on the sides of the case.

151

SHELVES

SHELVES may be made from solid wood, plywood, glass, or one of the man-made materials. But, no matter what their substance, they must be thick enough to keep from bending under weight. Their depth and spacing are determined by the overall dimensions of the particular unit into which they will be fitted, yet the spacing should be convenient and should make the best possible use of the available area. Construction may be stationary or adjustable; however, adjustable arrangements are considered to be more flexible and efficient as they can handle changing conditions.

Standard *book* shelves are eight or ten inches deep with the upper shelves being nine and one-half inches high and the lower shelves being twelve and one-half inches apart. Shelves in a *china cabinet* usually have a groove cut from one and one-half to two inches from the back edge so that dishes can be displayed in an upright position.

TOPS

For many pieces of furniture, the TOP is made as a removable part and is installed after the other construction is completed. It is made from the

choicest cuts of the wood, the pieces with the most beautiful grain. The edges are refined with a simple square cut, an undercut chamfer or rounded shape, or a molded design.

TAPLE TOPS are fastened directly to a leg assembly. Table top fasteners or clips are used for solid tops while special methods are needed for sectioned tops.

DROP-LEAF TOPS have a stationary center section with hinged leaves on opposite sides. A long piano hinge or several butt hinges may be used to attach the leaves. When closed, the leaves drop down but extend beyond the top. To keep the leaf extended and rigid when it is being used, a support is necessary.

EXTENSION TOPS are cut across the center and are attached to extension slides fastened to the leg assembly. This allows the two sides to be pulled apart so that leaves can be added. Sometimes folding leaves are attached underneath on a special mechanism that lets the leaves be raised into position when the table halves have been separated.

CORNICES

CORNICES adorn the tops of high cainets and may be any type of decoration from a simple molding to a complicated unit with highly or-namented parts.

HARDWARE

HARDWARE is added to a piece of furniture to make it useful and to complete the design. It is manufactured in many styles: Early American, traditional, contemporary, Spanish, and French and Italian Provincial. The quality and finish vary, and there is a wide selection among the different types in both size and shape.

HINGES are joint devices that allow a door to swing.

KNOBS or PULLS are handles usually with a round shape.

CATCHES are holding devices that keep doors in position. They consist of two pieces: one that is fastened inside the door and the other that is fastened to the inside of the cabinet. When the door is closed the two pieces interlock to keep the door from moving. The catch may obtain its holding power by magnetism, friction, or rolling.

LOCKS are mechanical devices with a bolt, and usually a spring, that are secured in place with a key.

SUPPORTS are special mechanisms for holding sections of furniture in a desired position. These are usually used with table tops and leaves; however, some desk tops and other special pieces of furniture may also require them.

CASTERS are small wheels or freely rolling balls set into a swiveled frame and attached to the legs or corners of furniture so that they can be easily moved.

SLIDES are narrow tracks fastened to drawers and some table tops to allow them to move easily and freely.

GENERAL HARDWARE REQUIREMENTS

DOORS
HINGE:	hinges, pulls, catches, locks
DROP:	continuous or piano hinges, lid supports (chain or folding hinge), catches, locks, pulls

DRAWERS	slides, pulls, locks
TABLES	table top supports, drop-leaf hinges, drop-leaf supports, leaf addition mechanisms
CHAIRS	casters
CABINETS	shelf hardware
SCREENS	double-action hinges

CHAIRS

A CHAIR is the most difficult piece of furniture to design and build as it is a collection of shapes and angles with few right angles between the parts. The back is narrower than the front with the back and seat usually shaped or contoured. The back legs are arched or angular and are wider apart at the top than at the bottom, and the stretchers may have a slight arc.

Chairs are put together with leg-and-rail construction. The seat may divide the leg assembly and the back and/or arm sections, with both units being fastened into it.

THE CUSTOM SHOP

The custom shop creates fine furniture from wood. However, the mainstay of any custom shop is service. The craftsman works with the designer discussing and planning all of the details pertinent to the design and construction of a unit. Often, the designer has a preconceived idea about the type of piece he needs. He can submit scale drawings, sketches, prints, pictures, or photographs of an item and the craftsman will work out all of the details and produce working drawings. From these drawings, the article will be executed.

The artisan can offer solutions to difficult design problems as a piece must be structurally sound as well as beautifully styled. His expertise will help him to judge whether or not a design or construction change is warranted to render a piece valid. He can suggest methods for improving structural fallacies by indicating alternative construction techniques and design changes. In this way, he can effect compromises between design and construction that will minimize problems and enhance the visual aspect.

Also, if it is desired, the craftsman will design an item to fit a particular need. This can be easily implemented from the designer's specifications as to use, size, and finish; and it will result in an individualistic piece of distinctive design that may not be procured elsewhere.

Congenial communication is advantageous to both the designer and the craftsman. The designer must state his needs and preferences explicitly. Likewise, the artisan must, as openly, discuss methods and materials. Necessary changes should be considered and implemented as soon as possible. Such accessibility forestalls problems and misunderstandings.

It is preferable for a designer to indicate a funding allowance prior to discussing design. The craftsman is knowledgeable about material and labor costs; therefore, he can estimate a job accurately. He can also help generate a feasible design, one that can be constructed within the stipulated amount, yet one that will achieve the desired effect.

A craftsman sells his time and his talent. He bases the estimate for a job on time, plus materials, plus overhead, plus expenses, plus a mark-up or percentage profit. As with any business transaction, the artisan requires a purchase order from the designer. It is a record of the details — such as design, finish, size, etc. — that were agreed upon.

A designer should select a custom shop carefully. The names of reputable shops can usually be obtained from colleagues, and only those shops that are highly recommended should be retained. A reliable shop should be willing to discuss previous projects and have examples of its work for the designer to inspect.

The shop should be visited during the construction stages of an item. The piece can be inspected to see if it meets the specifications and if the ideas have been correctly interpreted by the craftsman. This kind of interest on the part of the designer will create good communications and result in a better job. Also, the responsibility for the project is shared.

It is good business practice for a designer to acquire some knowledge about furniture construction. An understanding of building methods will admit more comprehensive discussions and allow the preparation of valid specifications for the pieces to be made. Also, the designer will be able to distinguish good construction and workmanship from poor quality techniques and thus ensure that his client will have a valid piece with a sound structure and beautiful design.

CHAPTER 8   UPHOLSTERED FURNITURE

Definition and History of Upholstered Furniture
Frames
      Definition of a Frame
      Frame Sections
      Parts of a Frame
      Materials for Frames
            Wood
            Metal
            Plastic
Operations
      Webbing
            Definition of Webbing
            Types of Webbing
      Springing
            Definition of Springs
            Types of Springs
            Classification of Springs
      Rubber Webbing
            Definition of Rubber Webbing
            Types of Rubber Webbing
      Burlapping
      Edging
            Definition of Edges
            Types of Edges
      Stuffing
            Definition of Stuffing
            Kinds of Stuffing
            Understuffing
      Casing
      Padding
      Channeling or Fluting
            Definition of Channels
            Types of Channels
            Construction of Channels
      Tufting
            Definition of Tufts
            Construction of Tufts
            Methods for Tufting

Seats
    Types of Seats
        Pad Seats
        Spring Seats
Arms
    Arm Shapes
    Types of Upholstered Arms
Wings
Backs
    Types of Backs
        Pad Backs
        Spring Backs
    Construction of Backs
Coverings
    Definition of Covers
    Techniques for Covering
    Fabrics for Covers
        Durability
        Workability
        Weight
        Weave
Construction of Covers
    Banding
    Border
    Boxing
    Panel
    Welting
    Ruching
    Stretchers
    Decking
    Seat Covers
    Arm Covers
    Wing Covers
    Back Covers
    Outside Covers
    Dust Covers
    Skirts
    Trimming

Cushions and Pillows
    Definition of Cushion and Pillow
    Cushion Fillings
        Down
        Innerspring Units
        Foam Rubber
        Hair and Rubberized Hair
    Ticking
    Covers for Cushions and Pillows
Loose Cushion Upholstery
Recovering
Restyling
The Custom Upholstery Shop

UPHOLSTERED FURNITURE

UPHOLSTERED FURNITURE is a combination of materials — frames, springs, paddings, stuffings, and covers — that have been assembled in such a fashion that a comfortable seating surface is the result. It is a design and engineering collaboration that must be attractive to look at, supportive of the human frame, and sturdily built. Beyond this, it is an important item in every interior environment and must satisfy the needs of numerous individuals both aesthetically and practically.

HISTORY OF UPHOLSTERED FURNITURE

Fabric was originally used *with* wooden furniture as a decorative addition. Furniture was light and portable, and its embellishments were of a similar nature. Throws of rich and colorful materials were draped over seats, tables, and chests, and flat, squab cushions with large tassel handles were used on seats and chests or were placed conveniently on the floor.

During the fifteenth century, an innovation by Italian master craftsmen produced the first upholstery work. They fastened the fabric *on to* the frame of the chairs they built, shaping it to the form and fastening it with nails. This new method for covering seats created pieces of interesting and beautiful design, but the surfaces were stiff and unyielding.

Comfort became an important commodity in the next century. Upholsterers experimented with ways to soften seats and began adding dried grass, wool strips, and other stuffings under the cover. They also devised different shapes for the frame and the "square" styled chair was an important feature. It had separate seat and back panels that were upholstered and fastened to the frame with gilt or silvered nails.

Some important changes developed during the second half of the seventeenth century: French upholsterers created the sofa, and the armchair emerged. The stately elegance and imposing grandeur of the armchair embodied the styles and characteristics of the period. It had an unusually high rectangular back that was entirely upholstered, and the seat was exceptionally wide. Eventually, the armchair and the sofa were paired to establish the classical suite of drawing room furniture. These pieces were of a matching design which generally included wings and were covered with the same fabric. In fact, whole rooms of furniture, including stools and benches were upholstered "en suite."

A small, armless, upholstered chair was also very much favored during this period. It had a high, narrow back and short legs, and it could easily be moved about — down to the hearth to enjoy the warmth or into a grouping for games or chatting.

In yet another attempt to provide comfort, upholsterers began to change the shape of the frame. Straight lines and right angles were softened into curves more compatible with the human shape. Armpads were added to the wooden arm, and fabrics of greater variety in color, design, and weave were used.

Around 1720, a wide, low, deep armchair was introduced. It had numerous forms, but it was made distinctive by its solid sides and loose cushion seat. Sofa shapes also began to diversify; some resembled large armchairs and others were elongated to accommodate three persons. These had a long, loose seat cushion and pillows at either end.

Another design for seating — the daybed — also appeared. It was produced in an assortment of sizes and styles with gondola-shaped backs, sectionals in two or three parts, or chair ends with deep upholstered wings. Others had ends of equal height or sloping backs that were considerably higher at the head end. As the daybed user was in a semireclining position, cushions and pillows were added to give greater comfort.

About the middle of the eighteenth century, the greatest revolution in upholstered furniture occurred — coil springs were introduced. Carriage seat springs were used in the beginning. They were nailed into wood slats that were then fitted into the seat frame. Horsehair padding was placed over them and the cover was fitted around the entire unit.

As time passed, coil springs expressly designed for furniture were perfected. Padding underwent a series of improvements as well and is now divided into two categories: padding and stuffing.

For centuries, upholsterers have labored to create beautiful and artistic surfaces for sitting. Styles have ranged from plain covers to rich fabrics with deep tufting and lavish ornaments to the simple elegance of the modern form. But the common objective for all upholstered furniture has always been to provide *comfort* for the user.

FRAMES

The FRAME is the understructure of an upholstered article. It defines the basic shape of the piece and establishes a foundation for the design. Even more importantly, it provides support and comfort for the user.

Frames are composed of several sections — SEATS, ARMS, BACKS, and WINGS. Each of these components comes in various sizes and shapes and may be put together in almost limitless combinations. Thus, although there are only a few basic frame designs, numerous and distinctive styles can be created.

The parts of a frame are termed supporting members or upholstery pieces. SUPPORTING MEMBERS are those elements that create and strengthen the frame and include the seat, top, and wing rails; the legs; and the front, back, and wing posts. UPHOLSTERY PIECES shape and hold the upholstery materials and consist of slats or uprights, underarm strips, and liners or tack rails.

Frames must be well built if they are to endure. They may be constructed from kiln-dried, straight-grained, SEMI-HARDWOODS that are free of knots and that are cut in widths of one and one-eighth to one and one-half inches. Generally, these are alder, birch, magnolia, mahogany, maple, and oak. Such woods have the strength and density necessary for upholstery purposes, yet they are easy to work with because they are light.

Members for wood frames must be precisely cut so that the joints have a tight fit. To ensure permanence, the joints should be secured with double dowels, glue, and corner blocks. Corner blocks are especially important in the seat as they give support to the legs, a reinforcement necessary to prevent the legs from splitting the frame. They should be solid blocks of wood about two inches thick, shaped to fill a corner completely.

Frames may also be made from METAL — tubular, square, or flat bars of aluminum or a steel alloy. The joints are permanently united with welding or brazing, and the legs are attached in the same manner. As metal frames are not only structural members, but are design or accent

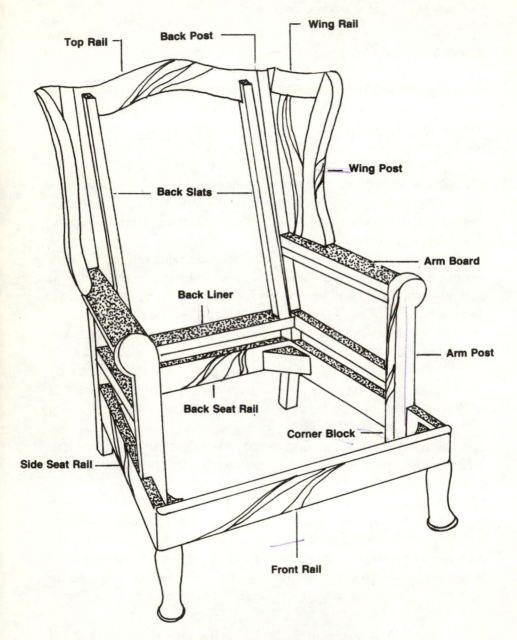

Top Rail

Back Post

Wing Rail

Wing Post

Back Slats

Arm Board

Back Liner

Arm Post

Back Seat Rail

Corner Block

Side Seat Rail

Front Rail

Typical Upholstered Chair Frame

elements as well, they are left *exposed*. This requires that they be given finishes that will be compatible with the style of the interior. They are usually plated in bronze, brass, or polished chrome, or painted a color matching or constrasting with the upholstery fabric.

A third substance which is becoming important in the manufacture of frames is PLASTICS. Cast or molded plastics have inherent qualities that allow them to be used as materials for frame components or solid frames. First, they can be rendered with precision and attention to detail. Second, they have great durability and can withstand heavy usage. Solid frames are immediately ready for use. Plastic frame components are prepared for assembly and are put together in the same manner as a wood frame; that is, they must have mitered joints that are secured with an adhesive and corner blocks.

Categories for frame types are defined by their method of manufacture. These include open frames, solid base frames, slip frames, and exposed wood frames.

OPEN FRAMES consist of supporting members fastened together such that there are large cavities in the seat, back, and arms. They are made from wood, metal, and plastic.

SOLID BASE FRAMES are single pieces of shaped wood that are attached to the members.

SLIP FRAMES have a solid base or an open frame that is upholstered separately and attached to the article.

EXPOSED WOOD FRAMES have parts of the wooden frame that are not covered by the upholstery and that are given a fine wood finish, painted, or antiqued.

Most frames can accommodate the many different types of upholstery. However, some frames are better suited than others for certain styles. It is usually merely a matter of preference whether the upholstery is to be thin, moderate, or thick or if the cushions are to be solid or loose. When this decision is made, the correct frame can be chosen.

OPERATIONS

Regardless of the design, most upholstery jobs consist of the same procedures. These basic operations are fundamental to the construction of an upholstered piece and are necessary for its engineering. In their order of sequence, they are webbing, springing, burlapping, edging, stuffing, casing, and padding.

WEBBING

WEBBING is the base for most traditional upholstery. It consists of narrow strips of material that have been interlaced and fastened to the frame. This creates a durable yet resilient network upon which to build the

166

spring unit so that it will result in a comfortable, uniform seating surface. Its proper installation is essential for strong spring support and good spring action with a minimum amount of sag.

The most widely used webbing is tightly woven JUTE STRIPPING. Its usual width is three and one-half inches, but widths from two to four inches are also available.

WOODEN SLAT WEBBING is sometimes used in backs and seats instead of jute. It is especially suitable for deep seats which might otherwise require very large springs, as slat webbing can be set at any height in the cavity. There are drawbacks which must be considered, however. Wood does not have the response qualities of jute, and it can be noisy if it is not properly padded. For this type of webbing, the individual slats should be of hardwood, three-quarters to one inch thick and four to five inches wide.

Substitutes for webbing may be used in factory manufactured upholstery. These include metal straps, wires, or sheet webbing made from heavy jute cloth or woven polyproplylene. Such materials give good service and provide comfortable seats.

SPRINGING

SPRINGS allow an article to interact with the body. They contract in response to the amount of pressure applied, yet they retain their shape. They permit the sitting surface to be firm and comfortable, while supplying elasticity.

COIL SPRINGS, wires bent into a spiral shape, are the type generally used in upholstered furniture. They are manufactured in three shapes: conical, double helical, and cylindrical.

CONICAL SPRINGS have a smaller circumference at the bottom than at the top.

DOUBLE HELICAL SPRINGS are of equal size at top and bottom with the center or waist squeezed in.

CYLINDRICAL SPRINGS are the same width along their entire length.

The ends of a coil may be knotted to itself or left open. Securing the end coils of a spring strengthens it and eliminates any loose wires that might work through the upholstery. The ends may be treated alike — both knotted or both open — or only one end may be knotted while the other is left open.

Typical Seat Construction

Firmness is important to the efficiency of a spring. This is determined by the size and number of the coils, the overall shape, and the gauge and grade of the wire. Conical springs with only one large coil are firmer than others of comparable size. Double helical springs are rated as soft, medium, or hard according to the size of the waist coil. The smaller the waist coil, the firmer the spring.

Coil springs are classified according to their application and size and include upholstery springs, pillow or back springs, and cushion springs.

UPHOLSTERY SPRINGS, made of nine- to eleven-gauge wire, are the heaviest as they are used in the seats, the area that takes the most abuse.

PILLOW or BACK SPRINGS used in back and spring arms are of finer wire.

CUSHION SPRINGS, made from finer wire still, are usually fastened into inner-spring units for cushions, pillows, inside backs, and some thick inside arms.

Each spring is individually mounted on the webbing and hand tied into the frame. Generally, there are four rows of springs front to back, with close concentration in the other direction. The springs are fastened together with twine knotted in a four-way or an eight-way tie to create a functional unit. This means that each spring has four or eight ties holding

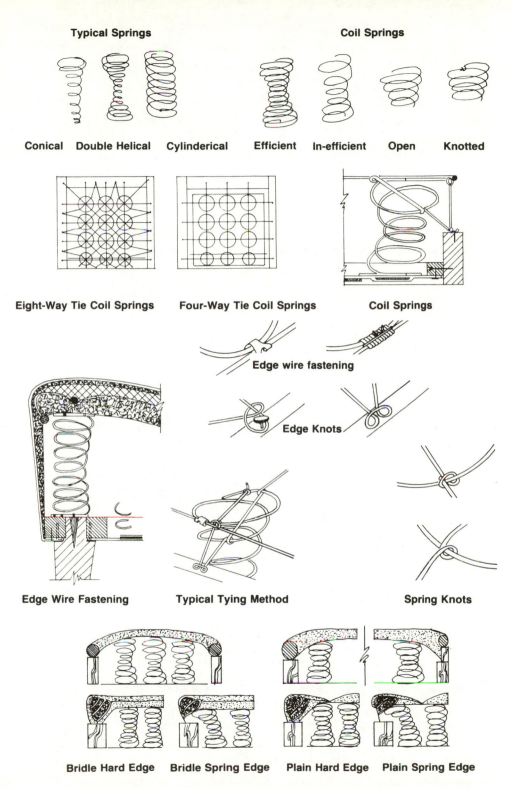

Typical Springs

Conical   Double Helical   Cylinderical

Coil Springs

Efficient   In-efficient   Open   Knotted

Eight-Way Tie Coil Springs   Four-Way Tie Coil Springs   Coil Springs

Edge wire fastening

Edge Knots

Edge Wire Fastening   Typical Tying Method   Spring Knots

Bridle Hard Edge   Bridle Spring Edge   Plain Hard Edge   Plain Spring Edge it in place. The number of ties depends on the desired firmness. The more knots holding a spring, the greater the support; therefore, an eight-way tie is firmer than a four-way tie. (This does not affect the longevity of the unit; both ties will last approximately the same length of time.)

EDGE-WIRES are put around the spring unit in seats and spring backs and are fastened to the springs as part of the four- or eight-way tie. They unite and shape the spring edges and help prevent the breaking or bending of the coil, a condition that could result in costly repairs.

ZIGZAG SPRINGS are wires bent into a series of short, sharp turns in opposite directions to form narrow, flat springs. They lie horizontally in the frame cavity and run from front to back. The ends are fastened to the frame with clips, and the edges are secured by ties. Adjacent strands are connected with small coil springs, wire links, or twine ties. This type of spring is especially suitable for thick and relatively flat surfaces. They are not bulky in themselves, and they do not require webbing, so the entire unit is very compact.

RUBBER WEBBING

RUBBER WEBBING is actually a combination material and can be classified as both strip webbing and springs. It is made of a double layer of textile cords that have been bonded together with pliable rubber. The cords run on the bias so that when the webbing is stretched, it will pivot toward the direction of the stretching. As the stretching is decreased, the rubber untwists and returns to its original shape. This characteristic contributes resiliency and allows the webbing to be used as a flat spring.

Rubber webbing becomes firmer and stronger the more it is stretched. The overall firmness is dependent on the type, width, and inital stretch as it is installed. All these factors affect each other and through this interaction provide a very versatile material that can be used for many kinds of jobs.

Several types and widths of rubber strip webbing are available. Maximum stretch may vary from forty-five to one hundred percent and widths may be as narrow as three-quarters of an inch or as wide as two and one-half inches. For best results, rubber webbing must be under permanent tension. This keeps it in place when there is little or no weight on it and returns it to its original position when a load has been lightened or lifted. The strips must be uniformly stretched for a smooth surface and a comfortable seat. It is attached to a wood frame with tacks or staples. Clips are also used, but these were made for fastening the webbing to metal frames.

This kind of webbing is generally found in cushion-type upholstery. It is especially suitable for thin, springy surfaces such as are needed in period pieces or antiques.

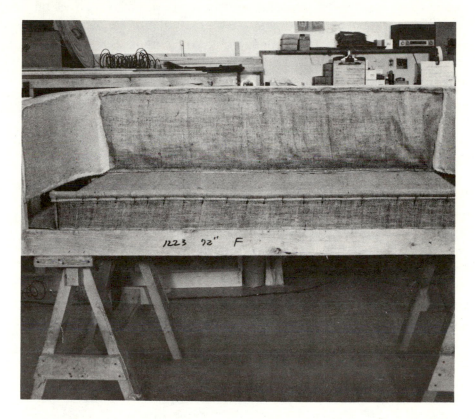

BURLAPPING

BURLAP, a coarse cloth made from jute, hemp, or one of the man-made fibers, is stretched across the springs or the webbing before the stuffing is added. It supports the stuffing and prevents it from working through the webbing or between the springs. It also provides a smooth base on which to shape the stuffing or to build upholstery edges.

EDGING

EDGES are added to upholstered surfaces that are to be loose-stuffed. The edges retain the stuffing, establish the desired shape, and supply a soft surface under the cover to protect it from wear.

There are three types of upholstery edges: roll, hard, and spring. The height of the upholstery edge above the rail determines which edge will be used.

ROLL EDGES are strips of burlap filled with loose stuffing. The burlap is rolled over the stuffing to give a rounded edge and to form a coil which may have a diameter to a maximum of one and one-half inches. The stuffing should be firmly packed so that the shape of the coil will be maintained. The burlap is tacked to the frame with cardboard stripping over it. The stripping holds the burlap tightly to the frame and keeps the roll edge stationary and neatly in place as the edge should be smooth with an even height and thickness along its entire length.

A prebuilt roll edging can be substituted for the handmade type. It usually has a jute, paper, rope, or cotton core which has been encased in felt or burlap. The diameter ranges in size from one-quarter to one-half inch, and the roll is permanently fastened so that it is ready to install.

HARD EDGES are built from the loose stuffing and the burlap cover. The stuffing is forced forward and is then locked in place by one or more rows of stitches sewed through the burlap cover. The stitching shapes the edge which must be well rounded. This type of edge is used for spring surfaces when the upholstery is to be one and one-half to three inches above the rail.

SPRING EDGES are necessary when the spring surface is more than three inches above the rail. They let the edge of the surface go down and rebound without permanent distortion. They utilize the coil springs and edge-wire in the seat to help shape the edge. The springs are covered with loose stuffing sandwiched between two layers of burlap. The top burlap layer extends over the springs to the rail and the stuffing is pushed into a rounded shape along the edge. It is held in place by several rows of stitching that go through the stuffing and the burlap and that are anchored to the edge-wire.

STUFFING

STUFFING is a soft, springy material that is added to a surface to form a pad. It should be durable, smooth, and resilient so that the cover will be protected. It is of major importance in upholstered furniture as it builds the shape and makes the sitting surface comfortable.

Two kinds of stuffing are used primarily — loose and compact.

LOOSE STUFFING consists of hairs or fibers that are unattached. The strands must be worked into position to build an area into a particular shape. The most generally used loose stuffings are horse and cattle hair, moss, palm fiber, cocoa fiber, sisal tow, excelsior, and tampico.

COMPACT STUFFINGS are polyfoam, foam rubber, or rubberized hair materials that have been formed into slabs or sheets. They are easily cut or bonded together to create a required shape and they can be readily built into smooth, symmetrical, consistent surfaces. They may be fastened to the desired area by bonding, tacking tape, tacking, or stitching.

FELTED PADDING is a matted cotton used as stuffing for thin, flat surfaces.

UNDERSTUFFING is extra stuffing material that is added to a surface to build a desired contour. It is usually made from loose stuffing or felted padding. Compact stuffing that is formed or trimmed to fit is also used.

Specifically, understuffing molds the CROWN which is the raised center of a surface. Crown augments the stuffing in pad and spring surfaces. It is necessary to make the casing uniformly tight, to minimize the packing of the stuffing, to improve the appearance of long and wide, flat surfaces, and to prevent the cover from pulling loose on spring surfaces. It must rise gradually from the edges toward the center and it must be firm, smooth, and evenly packed throughout.

CASING

CASING is a binding made from muslin or other similar materials. It envelops the stuffing, holding it in place. This simplifies the attaching of the cover and protects it from undue outward pressure.

PADDING

PADDING is a felted material made from natural staple cotton or polyester. It should be laid over all surfaces that are to be enclosed by a cover. It provides a smooth base for the cover as it hides imperfections in the stuffing and perfects the shape of the surface. It also dulls the sharp edges of the frame, eliminates any noises from loose stuffings and rubberized hair, and prevents hair and fiber from working through the cover.

CHANNELING OR FLUTING

CHANNELING or FLUTING is a decorative method for finishing the upholstery of backs and seats. It consists of grooves or furrows (channels) built into the stuffing as it is attached to an article. The channels should be about three to five inches wide at the midpoint and must be of uniform size and width. To maintain the shape, the crevices should be on fairly firm foundations and individual channels must be stuffed to the same density. The two channel types are end and closed.

END CHANNELS are those that finish with only one side against another surface.

CLOSED CHANNELS have both ends enclosed by other areas. Both types may be vertical or horizontal in direction. The number of channels is optional as is their placement, but they must be planned so that either a crevice or the center of a channel is at the middle of a surface.

Channeling materials include loose stuffing, fitted padding, and compact stuffing, plus muslin casing and the cover. To create channeling from these materials, three methods are used: muslin casing and cover, cover only, and channeled pad.

For MUSLIN CASING and COVER CHANNELS, a muslin casing the exact size of the channel is prepared. It is fastened to the surface beginning at the center, and, as each channel is attached, it is stuffed. A layer of stuffing is spread over each finished channel. Then the cover, which has been readied in the same manner as the casing, is installed channel by channel, beginning with the center and working outward.

The COVER ONLY CHANNELING METHOD is the same as the muslin casing and cover method, except the muslin casing is omitted. Special care must be used when forming the channels as they cannot be adjusted later without redoing the entire job.

CHANNELED PAD is a series of channels built on a base of burlap. When the pad is completed, it is tacked into the frame. It should be planned for a rather unyielding surface and an open frame.

TUFTING

TUFTING or DEEP BUTTONING is also a method for producing decorative upholstery work on backs and seats. It divides a surface into diamond-shaped sections by tying the four corners tightly so that a mound is developed. It is the most difficult upholstering style to produce as all tufts must be of regular size, shape, density, and firmness. Unless the tufts are precisely formed, they may be lopsided or lumpy.

To form a tufted surface, an article is upholstered through webbing, burlap, and basic shape. More stuffing is added to form the individual tufts. This may be a loose stuffing of curled hair or a compact stuffing of polyfoam or foam rubber. Stuffing is about one and one-half to two inches thick, but the thickness is dictated by the desired firmness.

Tufting points are plotted in relation to the size of a surface. Large surfaces have points four to six inches apart and smaller areas have them closer together. To create the diamond shape, points are placed on alternate rows and every other mark, in series. These patterns are flexible and should be based on the expected appearance of the finished piece.

There are two tufting methods: tufting by individual pockets or tufting a completely stuffed surface.

In TUFTING BY INDIVIDUAL POCKETS, the casing is fastened along two lines of points. The pockets are stuffed, then the next row of points are fastened and those pockets are stuffed. The work progresses in this manner until the entire surface is completed.

To tuft a COMPLETELY STUFFED SURFACE, the tufting twines are attached at the plotted points. The casing, with the tufting points marked, is laid over the surface and the twines are pulled through it. The casing is worked into place by tightening the twines gradually. When it is properly adjusted, the twines are tied.

In either case, the cover is put on after the tufts have been set. It is marked with the tufting points, and they are aligned with the surface points. Working from the center of the area, the cover is firmly pushed into the points and tacked into place. A cloth tuft or button is added to finish the point.

Tufting is often used with channeling to create an interesting surface. The area is channeled first and then the tufts are pressed into place. They are finished with cloth tufts or buttons.

SEATS

Upholstered seats are divided into two categories: pad seats and spring seats.

PAD SEATS consist of a foundation, stuffing, and casing. The foundation is either a solid base or an open frame with jute or rubber webbing. The stuffing may be compact or loose, but it is often felted cotton. Pad seats are usually solid cushion, that is, they are built directly on the frame or on a slipseat that is fastened to the frame after it is completed. These seats do not have springs and are not as resilient as those that include springs. They are divided into two types: flat pad and sag.

FLAT PAD SEATS have horizontal webbing and the stuffing lies above the frame.

SAG SEATS have depressed webbing that hangs below the frame. The cavity is mounded with the stuffing to make a comfortable cushion.

SPRING SEATS are built from a foundation, webbing, springs, stuffing, and casing. Generally, an open frame is the foundation for spring seat upholstery. It may have jute webbing and coil springs or rubber webbing may suffice for both. Loose or compact stuffing or a combination

of both are added to build shape and crown. The seat is encased in a muslin cover to hold the components in place.

There are two types of spring seats: solid and loose cushion.

SOLID SEATS have roll, hard, or spring edges added along the front and sides before the casing is attached. Then they are covered with the outside upholstery fabric.

LOOSE CUSHION SEATS have two distinct parts that are made individually and then placed one atop the other. These are the DECK whick houses the webbing and spring unit and the CUSHION itself. The cushion may be attached along the bottom surface to the seat cover.

ARMS

ARMS are developed from variations and combinations of several basic shapes. They may be FULL and extend the entire length of the seat, SET BACK so that the seat is T-shaped, or SCOOPED with an angular or curved notch cut out of the front. Armtops are patterned after one of the established types such as knife edge, modern square, rounded, square scroll, scroll, or T-shaped. The overall design is designated as straight, semicurved, or curved.

The durability and shape retention of an arm depends on the stuffing. It must be firm to hold the cover smooth, yet it must be resilient so that it will be comfortable. Both loose and compact stuffing are appropriate for arms and will produce the desired results.

Upholstered arms include the armrest pad, the covered armboard, and the fully upholstered arm.

ARMREST PADS are very small cushions that are attached to an exposed wood arm to make it more comfortable. They are built from stuffing that is installed on the armboard, covered by casing, and stitched to form a smooth regular shape.

COVERED ARMBOARDS are the upholstered tops of exposed wood arms. This may be several layers of felted padding held together by the cover if the stuffing is to be one-half inch thick or less. Otherwise, the surface may be outlined with edging, filled with loose or compact stuffing, encased in muslin, padded, and then covered.

FULLY UPHOLSTERED ARMS have four parts — face or front, outside, top, and inside — that are completely covered with fabric. Roll edges or prebuilt edging is used if the thickness of the upholstery requires it, and it is installed first. The inside arm is webbed, usually with a few vertical strips of jute or rubber webbing, and then burlapped. Armtops are built with loose or compact stuffing held in shape with bur-

lap. The armtop and inside arm are stuffed with loose or compact stuffing, depending on the shape, and the entire arm is encased in muslin, and covered with the upholstery fabric.

WINGS

WINGS are any part of a chair attached to the front or side of a back above the arm. Their overall shape is subject to many variations. Posts and rails may be flat, arched, or scooped in design as well as being straight or inward or outward curved. Their general form depends on the style which may require that they be rounded, square edge, or knife edge. Because of their small size, they are usually finished plain.

The frame for a wing may be open or solid base. Webbing is seldom necessary in wings unless the cavity is more than seven inches wide. In that case, two webbing strips running parallel to the back post or line, are sufficient. Usually the wing cavity is simply filled or covered with burlap. Edging is added if it is needed and then the stuffing is applied.

Stuffing choice is based on whether the wing is to be used for comfort, decoration, or both. Comfort demands a softer stuffing, but as a wing is generally decorative, the stuffing only builds and holds the shape. Either loose or compact stuffing is suitable and will fulfill the requirements.

Encasing wings in muslin is not mandatory unless loose stuffing is used or the wing is large. Then muslin is needed to establish the shape.

BACKS

The upholstery methods for backs are the same as for seats except that the materials are softer. Like seats, backs may be either pad or spring upholstery. The choice is a function of the frame as well as the design, as some frames accommodate both, while others are suited to only one. Pad upholstery is preferable as springs may make the seat too shallow. If springs are desired, rubber webbing can be substituted.

Stuffing is a component of major importance in backs and may be of either the loose or compact variety. Loose stuffing is appropriate, but care must be taken to ensure that it will be spread smoothly. Compact stuffing is excellent as it will always build a smooth surface.

Webbing is added to back cavities to give support even though backs are subject to less weight and pressure than seats. It should follow and maintain the shape of the back frame for maximum results. Both vertical and horizontal strips can be used, but they must be attached to

correspond to the frame type. Jute or rubber webbing are generally chosen, but wooden slat webbing may be practical for certain designs.

The inner surface of the finished back establishes the depth of the seat. This DEPTH is the distance from the back to the front of the sitting area. It should be sixteen to twenty inches for upright sitting and twenty-one to twenty-five inches for lounging.

The TILT or PITCH of the back defines the comfort of the seat. It is built into the frame and is maintained by the surface of the inner back upholstery. The stuffing, springs, or both can be placed so that the built-in pitch or the seat depth will be changed.

Inside backs are built as solid, loose pillow, or attached pillow.

SOLID BACKS are the pillowless type that have a neat, tight cover. This is a versatile design that can be used on any shape.

LOOSE PILLOW or PILLOW BACKS have a thin, solid back that supports an unattached pillow or cushion which is completely upholstered.

An ATTACHED PILLOW BACK is a solid back upholstered to give the appearance of a loose pillow back.

COVERINGS

COVERINGS are the decorative fabrics used to upholster the outside surfaces of furniture. They finish and beautify a piece so that it will be an attractive addition to a room.

TECHNIQUES FOR COVERING define the many methods for making an article distinctive. They allow artistic talent to create unique pieces that will fulfill a specific need. Outside and inside covers may be of different colors, fabrics, or patterns. Skirts or flounces may be added or the fabric may be quilted to give richness and texture. Individuality may be displayed with large or decorative buttons, and accents can be provided with welts of contrasting color or material. Sometimes the cover fabric may even be used wrong-side-out.

There is a wide and varied selection of both natural and man-made fabrics that will be effective and durable. EFFECT governs the attractiveness of a piece. The dimensions of an article may be visibly changed by the fabric color, pattern or both. Stripes tend to widen and lower the look of an article if they are horizontal and to add height and reduce width if they are vertical. Pieces also seem larger if they are covered with bright colors or plain fabrics. Dimensions are least affected by moderately sized patterns or figures. Tufted and channeled surfaces require thoughtful fabric selection as scenes, figures, and even stripes can be lost in the crevices.

DURABILITY is a nebulous factor. Some materials remain new-looking for many years, while others look worn after a short period of time. Use is an important circumstance regarding wear; those pieces that will be used daily for many hours will need recovering more often than articles that are seldom used.

WORKABILITY is the quality of a fabric that allows it to be made into a cover. It is an important feature, as it affects the job and the final appearance of a piece. Each fabric reacts differently to the process of installation and only if such characteristics are taken into consideration will the job be of top quality. The properties that contribute to ease of handling include the weight of the material, weave and texture, and pliability and stretch.

WEIGHT is a rather arbitrary characteristic, but by dividing fabrics into weight categories, it is easier to distinguish which will be best for a particular job. Fabrics are classified by weight as light, medium, and heavy: Lightweight goods include broadcloth, chintz, cretonne, faille, muslin, moire, sateen, and silk. Medium weight materials are brocatelle, corduroy, damask, drill, gabardine, linen, monk's cloth, rep, satin, ticking, and twill. Heavyweight fabrics are brocade, velvet, chenille, crewel, frieze, leather, matelasse, quilted goods, tapestry, velour, velvet, and wool.

WEAVE, the way the threads are interlaced to form the fabric, constitutes another property that influences a fabric's ability to be manipulated. There are goods that can be easily shaped and fitted to a surface while others, stiff and inelastic, require meticulous working if they are to fit smoothly. Most fabrics hold the shape of the surface, but some will eventually sag or become permanently stretched. There are also those that will tear or ravel easily even with careful handling.

Another important consideration as to weave is the fact that it is usual for upholstery fabrics to have a TOP END. This is the direction from which the weave, pile, and design run. To ensure uniformity in the color and the pattern of the goods, the top end should be to or point to the top of the vertical surfaces: arms, wings, and backs; and to the back of horizontal surfaces: seats and seat cushions. If the fabric permits, the top end may also be laid to either side or RAILROADED. Railroading is a term that designates the placement of the fabric on an article when the length of the fabric runs from side-to-side rather than from top to bottom.

Stretch and pliability are important qualities of handling and appearance in a cover fabric. STRETCH is the ability of the fabric to be elongated in one or more directions when it is pulled and to be able to return to its original shape when released. It is necessary so that the fabric can be made to fit over a surface and be manipulated into place. It also allows the cover to remain tightly fitted and securely attached.

CONSTRUCTION OF COVERS

The cover for an upholstered article consists of many sections sewn or tacked together over the frame. Most cuts are named after their associated parts, but there are additional cuts that are used with them.

BANDING is a narrow piece of goods, with or without welt, that is *sewn* into place *by hand*. It covers the spring edge portion of a seat and extends from the edge-wire to the rail or under it. It shapes the spring edge and reduces the puffiness of the side when the seat is used. This lengthens the life of the cover and improves its looks.

BORDER is a strip of fabric, with or without welt, that has one or both sides *tacked* to the frame. Its functions are the same as banding; only its method of installation is different.

BOXING is a thin section of material, with or without welt, that is *machine sewn* to a cover. It accommodates the edges of surfaces and allows a cover to be formfitting.

PANEL or FACING is a strip of goods, with or without welt, that is *tacked* over a piece of shaped board which, in turn, is fastened to the frame.

WELTING is a very narrow piece of cover fabric that is sewn over a filler cord. It is a single band inserted in the seams where the cover is sewn together. It is essentially a decoration and enhances the appearance of the finished cover; however, it is an optional addition.

DOUBLE WELT has two filler cords sewn into one cover strip such that twin rows of welt result. Because of its unusual shape, it is glued into position. Double welt made from fabric cut on the bias is usually flexible enough to be worked into most corners. However, it may fit in sharp angle corners better if it is cut and joined. It is usually added along the edge of an exposed wood surface.

SELF WELT is made as part of the boxing by turning the top and bottom edges over a filler cord and sewing them in place. It is used primarily with striped fabrics as it permits a perfect alignment of the stripes.

RUCHING, a pleated trimming, may be inserted along an outside edge. Since it should stick up or jut out from a surface, it is most often used along the top and sides of an outside back. It is made of a double thickness of the cover fabric or a contrasting or matching material that is box pleated with no gaps between inside and outside pleats. After being installed, it is banded by welt, then the outside cover is attached.

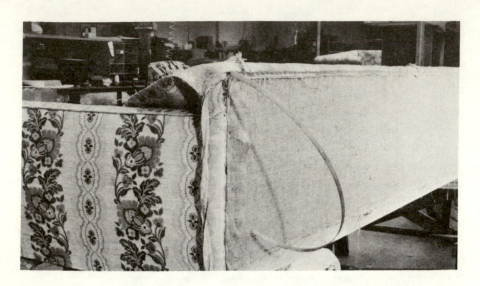

COVER STRETCHERS are pieces of strong but inexpensive fabric that are sewn to a cover to extend it beyond the point where it is visible. This is usually at a place where surfaces meet, and the stretcher is not seen when the article is completed.

DECKING is a section of goods used instead of cover material on the seat under a loose cushion. It extends from the back rail to the back of the hard or spring edge and runs across from one side rail to the other. As this area of a seat is not usually seen, there can be a considerable saving in cover cost.

On a SEAT, the cover envelops the largest section. A PULL-OVER COVER encases the seat *entirely*. It is made from a single piece of fabric that is stretched over the surface and fastened in place. A cover that will only partially conceal the seat is usually extended with banding, border, boxing, or panels.

ARM COVERS must be cut from the goods so that the design will match the fabric on the seat. Armrest pads, armboards, and partially upholstered arms may be cut from a single piece that is tacked in place and finished with double welt or gimp. Fully upholstered and some partially upholstered arms have inside and outside pieces that are assembled separately. Inside arms require stretchers at the bottom and back, and they are usually installed after the seat covers. Some styles may need border, boxing, or panels.

WING COVERS may originate from several sources. They may be individual items or extensions of both the inside and outside arm or back covers. They are usually a plain pull-around cover of a single piece, but they may be welted, bordered, or boxed.

BACK COVERS continue the design of the seat cover. However, inside back covers are the FOCAL POINT in the design as they are the sections that are most conspicuous. The placement of the dominant figure of the design must be carefully planned. A large, principal figure is usually centered and set closer to the top than the seating surface. Smaller, more regular designs run horizontally and are placed near the top of the inside back. Inside back covers are of two types: plain cover and those that are boxed, bordered, or paneled. A fully upholstered inside back usually needs stretchers on both sides and across the bottom.

OUTSIDE COVERS are attached after all inside covers have been installed. A layer of burlap should be fastened over all cavities to protect the cover by cushioning it against blows. The burlap and frame are shielded by a layer of padding which is also used to build any necessary crown. The sequence for securing outside covers is: wings, arms, and backs. Welting, panels, or both are added to the desired areas as the work on each section is completed.

DUST COVERS are the last "cover" pieces to be installed. They are placed on the underside of the seat to hide the upholstery materials and to help keep the inside clean. They also allow the article to "breathe" when it is depressed. Fabric for dust covers is either dark, glazed goods such as crinoline or cambric or a continuous filament material.

SKIRTS

SKIRTS are a decorative component to an article. They can alter the appearance of a piece by merely hiding the legs. But they can also change the total effect of an object by adding mass to the bottom, by making it seem broader and lower, or by drawing attention downward.

Skirts are usually made from the cover fabric. Variations are possible however, with contrasting colors and prints, such as a solid color skirt with a print cover or a figured skirt with a solid cover; stripes with solids and darks with lights.

Generally, a textile skirt is lined with muslin or sateen. Lining adds body which improves and maintains the shape of the skirt and gives it fullness. It also eliminates bulky hems and unsightly hemming stitches. Leather and plastic skirts are usually stiff enough without lining. Unlined skirts should have a hem at least one inch deep or more.

Skirts are installed after the dust cover has been attached. The top edge is often welted for a clean finish, but this is entirely a matter of choice.

There are three types of skirts: the flange, the box pleat, and the gathered or shirred.

FLANGE or STRAIGHT SKIRTS are strictly formal in style and are classed as traditional or modern. The outward appearance of both kinds is the same; the differences occur in the construction. The TRADITIONAL FLANGE is one continuous strip that is folded over itself to create the pleats. The MODERN FLANGE consists of individual strips that are laid over each other to *simulate* the pleats.

All flange skirts must have a simple, neat, tailored look. Pleats must be exactly placed — corner pleats at the corners and center pleats precisely in the center — and they must hang fairly straight. The bottom edge must be three quarters of an inch from the floor and the height must be exact on all sides.

The modern flange has certain advantages over the traditional. As it has fewer layers of material in the pleats, it is less bulky. This allows the pleats to hang more squarely and lessens puffiness.

BOX PLEATED SKIRTS are a general classification, neither formal nor informal. They consist of a series of inside and outside pleats that continue around the entire article. The pleats may be set in by one of three methods: inside and outside pleats meeting with no gap; inside pleats meeting but outside pleats having a gap measuring one-third the width of the outside pleat; or inside and outside pleats both having gaps measuring one-third the width of the pleats. Any method of pleating is satisfactory as long as the widths and gaps are uniform.

Pleats should be set so that they finish at the corners of the seat. Pleats without gaps must meet at the corners and those with gaps have the gap centered at the corner.

GATHERED or SHIRRED SKIRTS are a continuous piece of goods that has been ruffled across the top. Ruffles may be any size, but one-quarter to one-half inch deep is usual. The gathers are evenly distributed along the piece and then the skirt is attached to welt to hold the ruffles in place.

TRIMMING

TRIMS finish an article and give it a professional appearance. They include buttons, gimp, fringe, double welt, and antique and trim nails. They are available in many different sizes, shapes, colors, designs, and materials.

BUTTONS have two functions on an upholstered article. They may be utilitarian and hold the cover in place, or they may be merely decorative. Decorative buttons cover the edges of the pleats in a scroll and divide large, plain surfaces into more eye-appealing areas.

Buttons are made from plywood, plastic, pressed fiber, or heavy cardboard forms. The forms are encased by the cover fabric or by harmonizing or contrasting goods. Buttons may be secured by twine, tacks, or nails. Those anchored by twine must be installed prior to the outside covers. Tack- or nail-held buttons are hammered in place after the upholstering has been completed.

GIMP is used on articles that have exposed wood surfaces to hide the edges of the cover and the upholstery tacks. The best method for applying gimp is glue as it holds the entire strip to the surface and prevents the edges from curling or tearing. Because it is soft and flexible, it can be glued in a continuous strip around contours and corners.

FRINGE may be substituted for welt on certain parts of an article. It must be used with some discretion, as too much fringe makes an article seem lumpy. Fringe on inside cover pieces is usually machine sewn into place. It is tacked or handsewn on outside cover areas.

ANTIQUE and TRIM NAILS are added to articles with exposed wood surfaces. Usually, the edges of the cover are gimped before the nails are driven into place. They may be set any distance apart, but the spacing must be consistent.

CUSHIONS AND PILLOWS

Cushions and pillows are pads added to a seat to make it softer and more comfortable. They should fit snugly into the seat and blend into its design. Their construction is based on the cover goods, the filling, and the method of installation. And, the life, looks, and comfort of a cushion or pillow are a result of the construction process and the filling.

A pad put down on a seat is referred to as a CUSHION, and a pad placed against the inside back is designated as a PILLOW. The cushion usually extends to the inside back with the pillow resting on top of it. However, a pillow may rest on the deck as well. The cushion should align with the front edge of the seat, while a pillow rises an inch or more above the back.

Pillows and cushions are built from a cover, casing, and a filling. Their type is determined from the filling and the pillow or cushion is referred to in this way. Any filling may be used, but one may be more appropriate than another, so the choice usually depends on the style and the design. Typical fillings include down and feathers, innerspring units, foam rubber, and hair and rubberized hair.

DOWN is the light, fluffy filament growing from the quills under the feathers of an adult bird. It makes a durable and soft filling, but it does not

hold a shape well. To overcome this, it is strengthened by adding feathers, preferably goose. Down and feathers are used alone as pillow filling, but if they are to be used in a cushion, innerspring units or foam rubber are used with them.

INNERSPRING UNITS are groups of cushion springs that have been individually encased in muslin and fastened together. They are durable and rather soft, but to obtain a particular feel, they are often wrapped with other materials such as polyfoam, foam rubber, or polyester before they are bound in the ticking.

FOAM RUBBER unites the qualities of down and innerspring units to supply a filling that is soft, durable, and shape retentive. For maximum service, foam rubber should be wrapped with felted padding.

HAIR and RUBBERIZED HAIR produce a firm, flat pad that is especially suitable for benches and window seats. They are usually overlaid with felted padding so that the surface will be smooth.

Small pieces of fillings may be fine enough to work through the fabrics used for coverings or the stitchings of airtight cover materials. To keep these contained, special fabrics called TICKINGS have been developed for most of the filling types. Ticking also acts as a buffer; it helps the stuffing retain its shape and keeps it from breaking down.

PLAIN TICKING covers, which are merely casings for the filling, are adequate for small cushions; however, large cushions and most back pillows need partitioned ticking, and spring and down units require partitioned ticking pad.

PARTITIONED TICKING is a cover divided into six- to nine-inch sections by pieces sewn from side-to-side along the length. Each section is stuffed separately and then the entire ticking is closed.

A PARTITIONED TICKING PAD consists of two partitioned tickings joined by boxing. The spring and down unit is wrapped in felted padding and then inserted between the pads.

COVERINGS are cut so that the design in the fabric will match or harmonize with the cover on the seat and inside back. CUSHION COVERS are usually boxed and finished with welt or fringe. The welt may be prepared and then sewn to the cover or, if it is more practical, self-welted boxing may be used. The boxing along the lower edge on the back of the cushion is left unseamed until the stuffing has been inserted and then it is blind stitched together. An alternative is to install a zipper, and this is often preferred as machine stitching appears neater than hand work. PILLOW COVER construction may be either boxed or seamed and, quite often, it is both. In the latter case, the front and back covers are seamed together at the top while the sides and bottom are boxed. Welt or fringe may be added but these are an option of the design.

If a pillow or cushion is to be covered with an airtight goods like leather or plastic, a vent must be installed to allow the air to move freely in and out. "Breathing" inhibits seam splitting and retards shape change. Two kinds of vents are used: a wire mesh material set in large eyelets or grommets, or a casing made from a coarse fabric such as denim. The fabric vent makes a quieter cushion as it stifles any wheezing noises that may emit around the airtight material.

LOOSE CUSHION UPHOLSTERY

Loose cushion upholstery makes a simple, practical, and comfortable type of furniture. It requires only a frame, some type of cushion support, and cushions. Because this is a specialized category of upholstery, some materials are more appropriate than others; but the design and construction still dictate the choice.

The frame is generally open for the back and the seat; a solid base frame might be too firm. Some type of flat spring is best suited for the cushion supports. This may be jute or rubber webbing, plain or spring-held metal strips, or elastic ropes. Cushions are basically firm as they are thin and are not eased by padding on the cushion support. The most common cushion fillings are foam rubber and polyfoam, although any filling can be used. They are often wrapped in one or more layers of polyester fiber to provide a softer sitting surface.

The covers for loose cushion upholstery are usually boxed on all sides, and welts and fringes may be used to finish the seams.

RECOVERING

RECOVERING is a relatively simple way to restyle an article. While it may be in good shape, an item may not blend into a new interior scheme, or it may be soiled. Pieces appear considerably different when the fabric or design of the cover is changed. Borders or boxing may be added or deleted as may trims and skirts. Usually, the recovered item can pass for a new one.

RESTYLING

RESTYLING creates a new piece of furniture from a still serviceable one. The one necessary resource is the ability to visualize the completed product. Once the ideas are crystallized, they can usually be accomplished through reupholstering or by altering the frame.

REUPHOLSTERING involves changing the shape of the upholstery on an article. Thin upholstery may be built up; thick upholstery may be pared down. A plain surface may be tufted or channeled; three-dimensional surfaces may be made plain. Rounded arms or backs may be squared; elaborate designs may be tailored.

ALTERING THE FRAME may be necessary to achieve the desired result. It is the most extensive method, but also the most effective. If a frame is in good condition, additional rails and posts may be attached to produce the new shape.

Seats are restyled to make them more comfortable or as a result of a change in the type of upholstery. One of the most common modifications in seats is deepening, that is, increasing the distance from front to back. Seats are also heightened — raised several inches from the floor — or lowered two or three inches closer to the floor. Lowering does not change the seat height; it merely means that another row of rails and shorter legs will be installed.

Arm restyling alters the overall appearance of a piece more dramatically than any other change. Usually, wood is *added* to the frame for reshaping, as cutting tends to weaken it. Arms may be reshaped from set back to full or scooped arm, from scooped to full arm, and from scroll to modern square, T-shaped, or square scroll arm. They may be widened to add mass or to give the effect of lowering the back. Also, they are heightened, filled in, or changed from straight to curved.

Wings are often added or removed entirely. Their shape can be modified only slightly and is usually limited to filling in scoop or building greater scoop to upper and front surfaces.

Back restyling is accomplished by heightening, lowering to add bulk, widening to improve appearance, or thickening to allow better spring action. Backs may also be reshaped by squaring, scooping, or arching. Open-frame pieces may be filled in and converted to a fully upholstered style.

THE CUSTOM UPHOLSTERY SHOP

Most metropolitan areas have upholstery shops to assist the interior design profession. These shops do custom work in the building of new pieces and the recovering and restyling of others. They offer a very important service, as a custom job may be the only solution to a difficult design problem.

The distinctive commodity of the custom shop is individuality. A client employs a designer to provide for his personal needs. These may be physical characteristics such as height, weight, or incapacity; or they may be the particular tastes of color, style, or shape. The custom shop will work with the designer to correlate all the elements into a beautiful and satisfying piece. Their collaboration will result in a fine piece of furniture, original in design and skillfully and expertly executed.

The technical aspects of the job are handled by the shop. A qualified representative will take all measurements following the standard procedures. Free-standing pieces must be measured on all surfaces and built-ins require templates cut to the exact shape of the sites where they will be installed.

A list of materials is developed after the design and measurements have been determined. The shop supplies the frames, webbing, springs, stuffing, padding, casing, nails, glues, and trims. The designer generally orders the cover fabric using the yardage recommendations of the shop.

A sample of the cover fabric should be submitted to the shop for appraisal. Each fabric has its own characteristics and these must be assessed before deciding yardage amounts. Distinctive features such as stretchiness, raveling, widths, and pattern repeats are important considerations as they can dictate cutting methods, seam locations, and placement on the item.

To build a piece of quality workmanship and construction takes time. The time allowance is usually five to six weeks, but this number is flexible. Special handling may be necessary with certain jobs, so the time is reduced, but this is not the normal method.

The shop should advance a detailed statement for material and labor costs prior to the commencement of the work. The designer and the client are entitled to this courtesy, as most jobs have funding ceilings to consider.

CHAPTER 9   **ACRYLIC FURNITURE**

History of Acrylic Furniture
Definition of Acrylic Resin
Construction
Features
Molded Plastic Furniture

The beginnings of acrylic furniture rest in the evolution of plastic. The founder of the plastics industry was the English inventor Alexander Parkes. He discovered "celluloid," the oldest plastic, and acquired a patent on it in 1855. He also produced "parkesine," another type of plastic, about which he was asked to read a paper to the Society of the Arts on December 20, 1865. Celluloid was ultimately developed commercially, but not until late in the nineteenth century. The first commercial plastic, cellulose nitrate, was marketed in the United States in 1868.

The next innovation did not appear until 1909 when Dr. Leo Henrik Bakeland created phenolformaldehyde resins. Bakelite, a plastic whose trade name was derived from Dr. Bakeland's name, was the first phenolic in the United States. Only two additional plastics, cold molded and casein, were introduced during the next seventeen years, but after this time plastic production intensified.

In 1927, cellulose acetate became available. Initially, it was manufactured only in sheets, rods, and tubes; then in 1929, a new type in the form of molding material was evolved. This was the first injection-molded plastic. Acrylics appeared commercially in the United States in 1936, with polyethylene, an English discovery, and the polyesters in 1942, and polypropylene in 1957.

After World War II, furniture designers began to look into the possibilities of plastics as furniture materials. It was found that they had to be reinforced to provide a strong enough substance, but their molding properties held the key to a shape that would be form fitting, to provide greater comfort for the user, and that would be graceful and fluid in design as well. Eero Saarinen, an architect-engineer, was the pioneer in this medium. In 1946 he presented an armchair with a molded plastic shell that was upholstered with foam rubber and cushioned on both the seat and the back. It sat in a cradle-shaped framework of tubular steel that was mounted on four steel legs. He also designed a chalicelike chair which he introduced in 1956. It had a single stem and base unit of spun aluminum and a molded plastic shell that had been reinforced with fiberglass.

Arne Jacobson, another designer, worked in the medium too. He produced a chair with a resinous plastic shell standing on a chromium-plated steel pedestal. It was upholstered with foam rubber and covered with hide or wool.

Up to this time, plastic had been an expensive material to work with. Strengthening agents had to be added and much of the work could not be mechanized. With the development of polypropylene, a tough material that does not need reinforcing, injection molding could be applied to furniture making. The use of this technique was a significant advancement in the manufacture of chairs. It allowed a very comfortable chair to be produced at a minimal cost even though the initial investment for tooling was considerable.

Robin Day, working through a London firm, launched the mass production of injection-molded polypropylene seats. It was actually a stacking chair with a colored shell and a tubular metal frame. This chair was highly successful, and in less than a year it could be found in almost every country in the world. Eventually, Day also designed an armchair version of the stacking chair.

Other designers began to experiment with the new process. Don Albinson devised a stack and gang chair with separate pieces for the seat and back (1965). As the body rested, the pieces could "give" and therefore sitting was more comfortable. Joe C. Columbo planned the "Seggio" chair, the first four-legged chair that was made completely by the injection-mold process (1967). Eero Aarnio used reinforced fiberglass for his interesting contributions. The "Gyro" chair was egg shaped with two molded parts entirely of plastic, put together so as to allow a rocking motion. His "Ball" chair was an encircling shell of two molded plastic parts that were supported by a low metal base. Pierre Paulin designed the "Amoeba" chair and Verner Panton's chair employed cantileverage to balance the sitter's weight.

As was to be expected, the use of plastics expanded to include other types of furniture. Anna and Giulio Castelli were the forerunners in this area with their firm, Kartell, near Milan, Italy.

DEFINITION

Acrylic resin has become an important material for the manufacture of furniture. It is an excellent vehicle for this purpose as it is a flexible, durable substance that lends itself to many treatments. Technically, it has unlimited versatility: it boasts the structural strength of steel while being light in weight, and it is shatterproof.

An acrylic resin that has been molded or formed into transparent or translucent sheets, tubes, rods, blocks, etc., is generally used for the construction of furniture. It has exceptional clarity and reflective characteristics, and it is especially effective when it has been twisted into shapes. No matter what its thickness, it is colorless. Yet it can be tinted with a variety of colors, and the quality of the color can be controlled so that it is consistent throughout the piece. Generally, the clear, waterwhite acrylic is preferred; and for this reason, it is produced in the largest number of thicknesses — one-quarter inch to four inches. However, there are one hundred forty-four different colors of acrylic on the market in one-quarter- and one-half-inch thicknesses, and other depths can be ordered.

Some acrylic is manufactured with a special surface feature, a coating that gives it the hardness of glass. This unique quality allows it to be used in many areas, but it is especially serviceable as a face material. This acrylic type is produced in several thicknesses.

CONSTRUCTION

To create a piece of furniture, the acrylic components must first be molded to the required shapes. This may be a shaping process subsequent to the original fabrication. Those pieces that are to be twisted are placed in large walk-in ovens which have been warmed for two hours to six hundred degrees. The acrylic is heated to two hundred and forty degrees and is then brought from the oven. Craftsmen wearing white gloves work it through a special machine that twists it into the desired pattern.

This machine, which took two years to perfect, has a complicated job to perform. As the acrylic is twisted, it shrinks in diameter as well as stretching in length. The machine must do likewise; that is, it must contract itself as it stretches itself as it twists the resin. Calculations for this process must be very exact. A predetermined finished length dictates the length of the piece to be heated. The diameter is specified by use: two inches for beds, three inches for tables, etc.

When all of the shaped components have been prepared, they are assembled using the appropriate fastening methods. There emerges a solid, sturdy piece of furniture bearing its own special characteristics.

FEATURES

With acrylic furniture, as with fine wood furniture, there are features that indicate quality. Most important among these are mitered joints and rounded edges. All edges should have the sharpness removed by softening the shape. Many edges are also beveled as this enhances reflectiveness. Beveling is usually only a slight angle with a slant from one-sixteenth to one-eighth of an inch.

MOLDED PLASTIC FURNITURE

Furniture in a great variety of shapes and sizes may be integrally molded of strong plastic. These are generally solid, complete pieces that have no joints or components. However, they may also be items that have a molded plastic piece as the major portion of their make-up.

This kind of furniture may be produced from polypropylene, a strong, rigid plastic that does not need strengthening. It is easily colored and has shiny surfaces that are stain proof, chip proof, and not easily scratched. Another basic compound for the manufacture of such furniture is polyester resin. This plastic is not as tough as polypropylene, and it must be reinforced with fiberglass or some similar material.

These materials allow furniture with great preciseness of design to be shaped. They can be molded to the body's contours to give a comfortable, supportive seat or they can be squared and angled into rectangular shapes for tables. The furniture made from them possesses unusual strength as a result of their solid construction. It also has a superior durability, as it is able to resist agents ordinarily destructive to wood.

BIBLIOGRAPHY

A Dictionary of Textile Terms. Danville, Virginia: Dan River Incorporated.

Allen, Phyllis S. *Beginnings of Interior Environment*. Provo, Utah: Brigham Young University Press, 1972.

Arnold, Pauline; White, Percival. *Clothes and Cloth*. New York: Holiday House, 1961.

Aronson, Joseph. *The Encyclopedia of Furniture*. New York: Crown Publishers, 1949.

Aronson, Joseph. *The New Encyclopedia of Furniture*. New York: Crown Publishers, 1967.

Banov, Abel; Lytle, Marie-Jeanne; Rossig, Douglas. *Wall Coverings and Decorations*. Farmington, Michigan: Structures, 1976.

Birrell, Verla. *The Textiles Arts*. New York: Harper and Row, 1959.

Boger, Louise A. *Furniture Past and Present*. Garden City, New York: Doubleday, 1966.

Collins, Peggie V.; Collins, Shirley W. *Putting It All Together*. New York: Charles Scribner's Sons, 1977.

Dal Fabbro, Mario. *Upholstered Furniture: Design and Construction*. New York: McGraw-Hill, 1969.

Dal Fabbro, Mario. *How To Build Modern Furniture*. New York: McGraw-Hill, 1976.

Davis, Frank. *A Picture History of Furniture*. London: Edward Hulton, 1958.

Dizik, A. Allen. *Encyclopedia of Interior Design and Decoration*. Los Angeles: Stratford House, 1976.

Editors of Time-Life Books. *Paint and Wallpaper*. New York: Time Life Books, 1976.

Educational Materials. Los Angeles: The Mand Carpet Mills.

Encyclopaedia Britannica. "Ebony," Volume 7, "Rosewood," Volume 19, "Spinning," and "Teak," Volume 21, "Textiles," Volume 22, "Weaving," Volume 23. Chicago: Encyclopaedia Britannica, Inc., 1945.

Encyclopedia of Incomparable Architectural and Decorative Windows, Doors, Dividers, Etc. Minneapolis: Pinecrest Incorporated.

Feirer, John L. *Cabinetmaking and Millwork*. Peoria, Illinois: Charles A. Binnet, 1967.

Gibbia, S.W. *Wood Finishing and Refinishing*. New York: Van Nostrand Reinholt, 1971.

Gilles, Mary D. *The Elegant World of Window Shades*. Cincinnati: Breneman, 1966.

Gloag, John. *A Short Dictionary of Furniture*. London: George Allen, 1969.

Held, Shirley. *Weaving*. New York: Holt, Rinehart, and Winston, 1973.

Howard Shutters. Sepulveda, California: The Woodmart.

Jessie Walker Associates. *How To Create Your Own Beautiful Windows Fashions*. Middleton, Wisconsin: Kuttner and Kuttner, 1971.

Katz, Laslo. *The Art of Woodworking and Furniture Appreciation*. New York: P.F.C., 1970.

O'Brien, Mildred J. *The Rug and Carpet Book*. New York: McGraw-Hill, 1951.

Parker, Page; Fornia, Alice. *Upholstering For Everyone*. Reston, Virginia: Reston, 1976.

Pegler, Martin. *The Dictionary of Interior Design*. New York: Crown, 1966.

Potter, M. David; Corbman, Bernard P. *Textiles: Fiber To Fabric*. New York: McGraw-Hill, 1967.

Schwartz, Marvin D. *Please Be Seated*. The American Federation of Arts, 1968.

Shea, John G. *Contemporary Furniture Making for Everybody*. Princeton, New Jersey: D. Van Nostrand, 1967.

Studio Dictionary of Design and Decoration. New York: The Viking Press, 1973.

The International Book of Wood. New York: Simon and Schuster, 1976.

The New Encyclopaedia Britannica. "Furniture and Accessory Furnishings," "Floor Covering History and Manufacture," Volume 7, "Plastics and Resins," Volume 14, Macropaedia, "Plastics," "Rugs and Carpets," Micropaedia. Chicago: Encyclopaedia Britannica, Incorporated, 1977.

Tod, Osma G.; Del Deo, Josephine C. *Rug Weaving for Everyone*. New York: Bramhall House, 1957.

Weeks, Jeanne; Treganowan, Donald. *Rugs and Carpets of Europe and the Western World*. Philadelphia: Chilton Book Company, 1969.

Windows Beautiful. Sturgis, Michigan: Kirsch Company, 1977.

Window Coverings. Gardena, California: Ohline-Carlton.

Window Magic. Los Angeles: Levelor Lorentzen Incorporated.

Wingate, Isabel. *Textile Fabrics and Their Selection*. Englewood Cliffs, New Jersey: Prentice-Hall, 1964.

Woven Wood: Idea Windows 2. Westminster, California: Liken Incorporated.

INDEX

Accordion doors for wood furniture, 149
Acrylic furniture, 193
    acrylic resin, 195
    construction, 196
    features, 196
    history, 194
Adhesives for wall coverings, 79
American Oriental rugs, 97
Arms for upholstered furniture, 177
    armrest pads, 177
    covered armboards, 177
    fully upholstered arms, 177
    shapes 177
Axminster weave for carpet manufacture, 90

Backing for carpets and rugs, 92
Backs in upholstered furniture, 178
    attached pillow, 179
    loose pillow, 179
    solid, 179
Banding,
    for upholstered furniture, 181
    for wood furniture, 148
Base in wood furniture construction, 145
Blackout draperies, 103
Blinds, 119
    color, 120
    components, 121
    definition, 120
    measurements, 122
    styles, 120
Border for upholstered furniture, 181
Boxing for upholstered furniture, 181
Brackets,
    for blinds, 121
    for curtain rods, 106
Braiding in textile construction, 53
Burlapping upholstered furniture, 171

Cabriole legs, 146
Café curtains, 103
Café rods, 105
Cane, 19
Canopies for woven shades, 126
Carpets and rugs, 83
    American Orientals, 97
    backing, 92
    color, 87
    construction, 89
      flat, 90
      pile, 89
    cushion, 93
    definition, 89

    fibers, 87
    history, 84
    installation, 83
    manufacture, 90
      knitting, 91
      tufting, 91
      weaving, 90
        Axminster, 90
        chenille, 90
        velvet, 90
        Wilton, 90
    Orientals, 95
Case construction for wood furniture, 146
    frame and panel, 148
    plywood, 148
    solid glued-up stock, 148
Casing for upholstered furniture, 173
Casting and molding plastic, 65
    compression molding, 65
    injection molding, 65
    liquid casting, 65
    low pressure molding, 65
    slush and rotational molding, 65
    transfer molding, 65
Chairs, 154
Characteristics of wood, 14
Chenille weave for carpet manfacture, 90
Cherry wood, 17
Color,
    blinds, 120
    shades, 116
    shutters, 131
    wall covering, 74
    wood 14,
    woven shades, 127
Coloring,
    plastic, 66
    wood, 24
      bleaching, 25
      natural, 24
      stain, 24
Components for blinds, 121
Cork wall covering, 78
Cornices for wood furniture, 153
Coverings for upholstered furniture, 179
    arm covers, 182
    back covers, 183
    banding, 181
    border, 181
    boxing, 181
    cover stretchers, 182
    cushions and pillows, 187
    decking, 182
    durability, 180
    dust covers, 183
    panels, 181
    ruching, 181

seat covers, 182
welting, 181
wing covers, 182
Curtain rods, 106
Curtains, 103
Cushion for carpets, 93
Cushions and pillows, 185
coverings, 187
down, 185
foam rubber, 187
hair, 187
innerspring units, 187
ticking, 187
Custom shop,
upholstered furniture, 189
wood furniture, 155

Decking for upholstered furniture, 182
Designs in wall coverings, 74
Doors for wood furniture, 149
methods for hanging, 149
flush, 149
lip, 149
overlay, 149
rolling, 149
sliding, 149
types, 149
flexible or tambour, 149
folding or accordion, 149
lightweight, 149
solid, 149
Double-hung draperies, 101
Draperies and curtains, 99
construction, 106
definitions, 100
hardware, 105
history, 100
installation, 111
styles, 101
workrooms, 111
Drawers, 151
Dyeing of fabrics, 55

Ebony, 15
Edging for upholstered furniture, 171
hard, 172
roll, 172
spring, 172
Exposed wood frames for upholstered
furniture, 165

Fabric
for shades, 116
for wall coverings, 78

Fabric construction, 42
braided, 53
knitted, 51
woven, 42
Fasteners for wood, 22
Fastening plastic, 67
Features of acrylic furniture, 196
Fiber, 33
man-made, 34
acetate, 37
acrylic, 35
aramid, 38
anidex, 37
azlon, 37
glass, 36
metallic, 37
modacrylic, 36
novoloid, 38
nylon, 36
nytril, 37
olefin, 37
polyester, 36
rayon, 37
rubber, 37
saran, 37
spandex, 38
vinyl, 38
vinyon, 38
natural, 33
cotton, 33
jute, 33
linen, 33
silk, 34
wool, 34
Filling for wood, 26
Films for wood, 26
lacquer, 27
linseed oil, 27
shellac, 26
varnish, 26
Finishing,
fabrics, 54
dry, 54
burling, 54
calendarizing, 54
gassing, 54
glazing, 54
napping, 54
scheinerizing, 55
shearing, 54
specking, 54
special, 61
absorbent, 61
antibacterial, 61
Fabric-to-fabric bonding, 61
Flame proofing, 61
foam laminating, 61

heat reflectant, 61
  mildew proofing, 61
  moth proofing, 61
  permanent press, 61
  shape retentive, 61
  slip resistance, 61
  wash and wear, 61
  water repellent, 61
  waterproof, 61
  wrinkle resistant, 61
  wet, 55
    dyeing, 55
    fulling, 55
    mercerizing, 55
    printing, 58
    scouring, 55
    soaping, 55
    souring, 55
  wood, 24
Flat surface carpets and rugs, 90
Flexible doors, 149
Flock wall coverings, 77
Fluting in wood furniture, 146
Foil wall coverings, 77
Folding doors, 149
Forming plastic, 66
  extrusion, 66
  powder molding, 66
  sheet forming, 66
Frames for upholstered furniture, 163
  materials, 163
  parts, 163
  types, 165
    exposed wood, 165
    open, 165
    slip, 165
    solid base, 165
Framing for blinds, 120

Grain in wood, 14
Grass cloth, 77
Groups of plastics, 64
  thermoplastic, 64
  thermosetting, 64
Guides and runners for drawers, 151

Hardness of woods, 14
Hardware
  draperies and curtains, 105
  shades, 117
  shutters, 131
  wood furniture, 153
Headings in draperies and curtains, 109
Hemlines in shades, 114
Hickory, 17

History
  carpets and rugs, 89
  draperies and curtains, 100
  textiles, 32
  upholstered furniture, 161
  wall coverings, 72
  wood furniture, 138

Inlay, 18
  banding, 19
  marquetry, 18
  parquetry, 19
Inserts for shutters, 130
Installation
  carpets, 23
  draperies and curtains, 111
  shutters, 131
  wall coverings, 81
  woven shades, 127
Interlining for draperies, 108

Joints, 20
  supports, 22
  types, 20
    butt, 20
    dado, 22
    dovetail, 22
    edge, 20
    lap, 22
    miter, 22
    mortise-and-tenon, 22
    rabbet, 20

Knit rug construction, 91
Knitting, 51
  fabric construction, 52
  stitches, 52
    plain, 52
    purl, 52
    rib, 52
    tuck, 52
  types of knitted fabric, 52

Laminate,
  plastic, 67
  wood, 19
Legs for wood furniture, 145
Length measurement for draperies, 107
Lightweight doors, 149
Lining,
  for draperies, 107
  for wall coverings, 79

Mahogany, 15
Maple, 16
Marquetry, 18
Measurements,
    blinds, 122
    draperies and curtains, 107
    quantity of wall covering, 80
    shades, 116
    shutters, 133
Metal wall covering (foil, mylar), 77
Molded plastic furniture, 197
Molding for wood furniture, 19

Oak, 16
One-way draw draperies, 101
Open frames for upholstered furniture, 165
Oriental rugs, 95
Orientalwood, 16
Overdraperies, 101

Padding for upholstered furniture, 173
Painting wood furniture, 28
    antiquing or glazing, 29
    distressed finishes, 29
    mottled finishes, 29
Panel for upholstered furniture,
Parquetry, 19
Pecan, 17
Pile carpets and rugs, 89
Plastic wall covering (vinyl), 77
Plastics, 63
    acrylic for molded plastic furniture, 197
    coloring, 66
    construction, 66
    definition, 64
    fastening, 67
    groups, 64
      thermoplastic, 64
      thermosetting, 64
    laminates, 67
    methods of fabrication, 65
      casting and molding, 65
      forming, 65
    polishing, 66
    resin board, 68
Pleats in drapery headings, 109
Plinth for wood furniture, 145
Plywood, 19
Polishing,
    plastic, 66
    wood, 27
      alcohol polishing or spiriting, 28
      French polishing, 28
      oil mixture, 28
      oil polishes, 27
      pigment oil/stain, 28
      qualasole, 28
      rottenstone, 28
Posts for wood furniture, 145
Printing,
    fabric, 58
    wall coverings, 76

Rails,
    frames for upholstered furniture, 163
    shutters, 130
Red gum, 16
Reeding on wood furniture, 146
Resin board, 68
Return on draperies and curtains, 107
Rods, 105
Rosewood, 15
Round legs, 146
Rubber webbing, 170
Rubbing for wood finishing, 27
Ruching for upholstered furniture, 181
Ruffled tieback curtains, 103
Rugs and carpets (see Carpets and rugs), 83
Runners and guides for drawers, 151

Satinwood, 16
Scallops for drapery headings, 109
Seats, 175
    pad, 175
      flat, 175
      sag, 175
    spring, 175
      loose cushion, 177
      solid, 177
Shades, 113
    colors, 116
    definition, 114
    fabrics, 116
    hardware, 117
    measurements, 116
    styles, 114
Shelves for wood furniture, 152
Shirring for drapery headings, 109
Shutters, 129
    color, 131
    construction, 130
    definition, 130
    hardware, 131
    installation, 131
    measurements, 133
    styles, 130
Skirts,
    upholstered furniture, 183
      box pleat, 184
      flange, 184

gathered or shirred, 184
woven shades, 124
Slip frames for upholstered furniture, 165
Solid base frames for upholstered furniture, 165
Solid doors for wood furniture, 149
Solid wood, 17
Species of wood, 14
Springing, 167
springs, 167
classification, 168
cushion, 168
pillow and back, 168
upholstery, 168
edge wires, 170
types, 167
coil, 167
conical, 167
cylindrical, 167
double helical, 167
zigzag, 170
Spring tension curtain rod, 106
Square legs, 146
Stains for woods, 24
chemical, 25
penetrating oil, 25
spirit or alcohol, 25
varnish, 25
water, 25
wax, 25

Stiles for shutters, 130
Strength of wood, 14
Stretchers for wood furniture, 145
Stuffing, 172
compact, 172
felted padding, 173
loose, 172
understuffing, 173
Styles of window coverings,
blinds, 120
draperies and curtains, 101
shades, 114
shutters, 130
woven shades, 124
Sugar knotty pine, 17
Surface types for wall coverings, 75

Tambour doors, 149
Teak, 15
Textiles, 31
braiding, 53
fiber, 33
finishing, 54
history, 32
knitting, 51
types of knitted fabric, 52

types of woven fabric, 46
weaving, 42
yarn, 41
Textile wall coverings, 78
Texture wall coverings, 77
Tiebacks in draperies and curtains, 103
Tops for wood furniture, 152
Traverse rods, 105
Trays for wood furniture, 151
Trim,
shades, 114
upholstered furniture, 184
woven shades, 127
Tripod legs, 146
Tufting in rug manufacture, 91
Tufts in upholstered furniture, 174
Turned legs, 146
Two-way draw draperies, 101

Underdraperies, 101
Understuffing, 173
Upholstered furniture, 159
arms, 177
backs, 178
channels, 173
coverings, 179
cushions and pillows, 185
custom shop, 189
definition, 161
frames, 163
history, 161
loose cushion upholstery, 188
operations, 165
burlapping, 171
casing, 173
edging, 171
padding, 173
springing, 167
stuffing, 172
webbing, 166
recovering, 188
restyling, 188
seats, 175
skirts, 183
trimming, 184
tufts, 174
wings, 178

Valances,
draperies, 103
woven shades, 124, 126
Velvet weave for carpet manufacture, 90
Veneer, 17
book matched, 18
burl, 18

butt, 18
checkerboard matched, 18
crotch, 18
diamond matched, 18
four-way center and butt matched, 18
inlay, 18
reverse diamond matched, 18
slip matched, 18

Wall Coverings, 71
adhesives, 79
amount of covering, 80
color and design, 74,
custom, 76
drop match, 76
straight match, 76

history, 72
installation, 81
lining, 79
sizes, 79
surface type, 75
types, 76
burlap, 78
cork, 78
flock, 77
metal (foil, mylar), 77
plastic (vinyl), 77
textile, 78
texture, 77
wallpaper, 76
Walnut, 16
Weaving, 42
basic weaves, 43
plain, 43
satin, 43
twill, 43
combination, 45
backed cloth, 45
basket, 45
double cloth, plycloth, pocketcloth, 45
jacquard, 45
lappet, swivel, clipspot, 45
leno, doup, 45
pile, 45
pique, 45
rib, 45
Webbing for upholstered furniture, 166
jute stripping, 167
rubber, 170
wooden slat, 167
Weights for draperies, 106
Welting for upholstered furniture, 181
Width measurements for draperies, 107
Wilton weave for carpet manufacture, 90
Window coverings, 99
blinds, 119

curtains, 99
draperies, 99
shades, 113
shutters, 129
woven shades, 123
Wood, 13
cane, 19
characteristics, 14
color, 14
coloring, 24
fasteners, 22
filling, 26
finishing, 23
grain,. 14
hardness, 14
joints, 20
laminate, 19
molding, 19
painting, 28
plywood, 19
polishing, 27
rubbing, 27
solid, 17
species, 14
strength, 14
types of wooden materials, 17
veneer, 17
Wood furniture, 137
chairs, 154
construction, 145
base, 145
case, 146
cornices, 153
doors, 149
drawers, 151
legs, 145
posts, 145
rails, 145
stretchers, 145
tops, 152
trays, 151
custom shop, 155
definition, 145
hardware, 153
history, 138
Workrooms, 111
Woven carpets and rugs (see Carpets and
rugs), 90
Woven shades, 123
colors, 127
construction, 127
definition, 124
installation, 127
styles, 124

Yarn, 41

CREDITS FOR PHOTOGRAPHS

Frontispiece

Interior Design by: Marjorie A. Bedell, A.S.I.D.
Photographer: George R. Szanik

Page 10

"Antique Kerman Laver"

Courtesy of: Vojtech Blau

Page 12

Interior Design by: Marjorie A. Bedell, A.S.I.D.
Photographer: George R. Szanik

Page 30

"Antique Aubusson" 18th Century Tapestry
Courtesy of: Vojtech Blau

Page 44

"Famatex Stentoring and Heat Setting Machine"

Courtesy of: Stead, McAlpin & Co., Ltd.
              Greeff Fabrics, Inc.

"Garden of Perfect Flowers"
Copyright © by Greeff Fabrics, Inc.

Page 50

Interior Design by: June Given, A.S.I.D.
Photographer: Max Eckert

Page 56

"Dye Machine"

Courtesy of: Webb Design Products

Page 58

"Buser Flat Bed Automatic Screen Printing Machines"

Courtesy of: Stead, McAlpin & Co., Ltd.
              Greeff Fabrics, Inc.

Page 60

"Stork 16 Color Rotary Screen Printing Machine"

Courtesy of: Stead, McAlpin & Co., Ltd.
Greeff Fabrics, Inc.

Page 60

"Brugmann Open Width Washing and Soaping Machine"

Courtesy of: Stead, McAlpin & Co., Ltd.
Greeff Fabrics, Inc.

Page 62

Courtesy of: The Swedlow Group

Page 70

"Pandjang"

Courtesy of: Albert Van Luit & Co.
Photographer: George R. Szanik

Page 82

"Just Desserts"

Courtesy of: Edward Fields

Page 86

"Antique Kerman Laver" (Vase Rug)

Courtesy of: Vojtech Blau

Page 88

Courtesy of: Bigelow Carpets
Photographer: Tony De Vito

Page 96

"Aubusson French Rug"

Courtesy of: Vojtech Blau

Page 98

Interior Design by: Penni Paul, A.S.I.D.
Photographer : Harold Davis

Page 134

Interior Design by: Marjorie A. Bedell, A.S.I.D.
Photographer: George R. Szanik

Page 136

"Philadelphia Highboy"

Courtesy of: Councill Craftsmen, Inc.
              James Davis & Associates, Inc.

Page 140

"Pembroke Table"

Courtesy of: Councill Craftsmen, Inc.
              James Davis & Associates, Inc.

Page 152

"Kyoto Table"

Courtesy of: Randolph & Hein, Inc.
              Kneedler-Fauchere

Page 155

"Thebes Chair"

Courtesy of: Randolph & Hein, Inc.
              Kneedler-Fauchere

Page 156

"Melanie"

Courtesy of: Albert Van Luit & Co.
Photographer: George R. Szanik ·

Page 158

"Chippendale Wing Chair;;

Courtesy of: Southwood Reproductions
              James Davis & Associates, Inc.

Page 166

Courtesy of: Martin/Brattrud, Inc.

Page 168

Courtesy of: Martin/Brattrud, Inc.

Page 171

Courtesy of: Martin/Brattrud, Inc.

Page 176

Interior Design by: June Given, A.S.I.D.
Photographer: Max Eckert

Page 182

Courtesy of: Martin/Brattrud, Inc.

Page 186

Courtesy of: Thonet Industries, Inc.

Page 190

Interior Design by: Craig Wright
Photographer: Max Eckert

Page 192

"Indienne"

Courtesy of: Albert Van Luit & Co.
Photographer: George R. Szanik

ABOUT THE AUTHOR

Dennis Grant Murphy, A.S.I.D., has a background spanning over twenty-five years in the profession of interior design.

He attended the Bisttram School of Fine Art and graduated from the Chouinard Art Institute with a major in interior design. He has served as Editorial Director of Architectural Digest magazine; President of the Los Angeles Chapter of the American Institute of Interior Designers; and Instructor of Interior Design at several colleges and universities in Southern California.

For nearly fifteen years Mr. Murphy was Executive Vice President of the Residential Interior Design Division as well as Operations Manager of five branch studios for Cannell & Chaffin, one of the country's most prestigious interior design firms. He is currently engaged in the practice of interior design and has authored a number of magazine articles on the subject. Additionally, he conducts seminars and appears as a guest lecturer at college and university campuses throughout the country.

Mr. Murphy's first book, *The Business of Interior Design*, is a required textbook in more than one hundred fifty colleges and universities in the United States and other countries.

Stratford House Publishing Company
P. O. Box 7077
Burbank, California 91510